FROM THE LOVE LANES OF LUCKNOW

Advance praise for the book

'Mehru Jaffer's captivating and picturesque account of Lucknow's romance with its classical Urdu poets magically transports us to the *mehfils* of Mir and Anis. Told in scintillating prose, interspersed with evocative and well-selected verse, it holds us in thrall compelling us to agree with Bismil's otherwise highly contentious claim.'

Kiya tabaah toh Dilli ne bhi bohot 'Bismil'
Magar Khuda ki qasam Lakhnau ne loot liya

—**Saif Mahmood**, author of
Beloved Delhi: A Mughal City and Her Greatest Poets

'Many mesmerising stories about Urdu classical poets circulate—wearing a veil of fact and fiction. To some extent, these stories are a part of our Urdu literary heritage. Even though scholars challenge the authenticity of these anecdotes, they cannot ignore their charm and their influence. Thank you, Mehru Jaffer *Saheba*, for bringing them to a wider audience.'

—**Timsal Masud**, lecturer, Hindi–Urdu translator, editor and textbook author, Middle Eastern South Asian and African Studies (MESAAS), Columbia University, New York

'Some cities are emblems. Lucknow is one such of its own tone and tenor, taste and touch in the broader domains of life and art. Mehru Jaffer brilliantly constructs this city where culture is carnivalesque and poetry a social rendezvous. She brings out the merits of *dabistaan-e Lucknow* with the unique mystique of *mushaira* and the finest marks of its poetry in *rekhta* and *rekhti*. This book is a marker of Lucknow's variegated histories, cultural cartographies and literary mythologies. While language found itself in the states of making and unmaking, and the socio-literary culture in flourishing and failing, Lucknow carved its own mythos of longing and belonging in life and art. This is just as Aatish did in terms of identifying the heights of poetic imagination and secularising language to configure the points of confluence between experience and expression.'

Zeena sabaa ka dhoondhti hai apni musht-e-khaak
Baam-e-buland yaar ka hai aastana kya

—**Anisur Rahman**, former professor of English, Jamia Millia Islamia, New Delhi, is the translator of 500 years of best Urdu poetry written by 65 poets, *Hazaaron Khwahishein Aisi: The Wonderful World of Urdu Ghazals* and *Hazaar Rang Shaairi: The Wonderful World of the Urdu Nazm*

FROM THE LOVE LANES OF LUCKNOW

An Ode to Urdu Poetry

MEHRU JAFFER

AMARYLLIS

AMARYLLIS

An imprint of Manjul Publishing House Pvt. Ltd.
• C-16, Sector 3, Noida, Uttar Pradesh 201301, India
Website: www.manjulindia.com
Registered Office:
• 2nd Floor, Usha Preet Complex, 42 Malviya Nagar, Bhopal 462 003 – India
Distribution Centres
Ahmedabad, Bengaluru, Bhopal, Chennai, Hyderabad,
Kolkata, Mumbai, Noida, Pune

From the Love Lanes of Lucknow: An Ode to Urdu Poetry by Mehru Jaffer

This edition first published in India in 2024

ISBN 978-93-5543-960-4

Cover design: Wasim Helal

Printed and bound in India by Parksons Graphics Pvt. Ltd.

For Iftikhar Arif,
whose passion for poetry and love for Lucknow is infectious

Contents

Mukhdon se patli raaj dulaari galiyan
Chauthi ki dulhan ki tarah pyaari galiyan
Dil ki nazariye se aah bharti guzrin kal raat ko
Lakhnau ki saari galiyan

—Unknown

More narrow than slim faces those beloved lanes,
Beautiful like a new bride those pretty lanes
Sighing with emotion, last night they passed by
All those lanes of Lucknow.

Lakhnau hai toh mehez gumbad-o-minar nahin
Sirf ek sheher nahi koocha-o-bazaar nahin
Iske aanchal mein mohabbat ke phool khilte hain
Iski galiyon mein farishton ke patey milte hain

—Yogesh Praveen (1938–2021)

Lucknow is not just domes and minarets
not just a city nor just a marketplace
In its lap the flowers of love bloom
In its lanes the abodes of angels loom discovered.

Foreword

Any mention of Lucknow conjures up images of a unique way of life practised for a little less than a century in Avadh. It is a journey back in time to the world of Nawab Asaf-ud-Daula, Nawab Wajid Ali Shah and to the city of Begum Hazrat Mahal, Mir Anees and of Majaz Lakhnavi.

Lucknow evokes poignant remembrances of *Indra Sabha* performances in Kathak style, the ghazals of Begum Akhtar, the footwork of Birju Maharaj—while simultaneously being the setting for *Shatranj ke Khiladi* and *Umrao Jaan*. The distinguishing feature of Lucknow is its reputation as the refuge of countless Urdu poets. I find it ironic that a settlement on the banks of River Gomti has gained fame as the cradle of a way of life called *Ganga–Jamuni*.

Urdu is the youngest language in the world, but the culture associated with it, especially its poetry, is unique amongst all the languages of the world. Urdu literary critics have contestably divided the poetry of the time into the Delhi School and the Lucknow School. In the Delhi School of Urdu poetry, critics find *dakhliyat* or internality, and in the Lucknow School is found *kharjiyat* or externality.

We are told that the spirit of one school is a perfect balance of art and craft. But a perfect balance of spirituality and materiality is found in all great Urdu poetry, whether it was written in Delhi or in Lucknow. For example, Zauq is from Delhi, but language is his forte. Aatish is from Lucknow, but he is best at internalising thoughts and feelings.

Reams have been written on the Delhi and Lucknow schools of Urdu poetry, especially by Abdul Lais Siddiqui on the Lucknow school and Dr Noorul Hasan Hashmi on the Delhi school.

A glance through the long list of poets who had once lived in Lucknow reveals how the life of every second person in the city had revolved around poetry, and poets like Mir Taqi Mir, Mirza Muhammad Rafi Sauda, Ghulam Hamdani Mushafi, Haider Ali Aatish, Imam Baksh Nasikh, Insha Allah Khan, Mir Anees, Daya Shankar Kaul Nasim, Agha Hasan Amanat, Wajid Ali Shah and Munshi Ameer Ahmad Minai were all pillars of the Lucknow school of poetry.

The river of poetry in Lucknow begins with *Burhan-ul-Mulk* Saadat Ali Khan, and flows down to Wajid Ali Shah. A glance through the reign of the rulers of Lucknow reveals the finest representation of Indo-Iranian culture in Avadh. The last phase of oriental culture was practised in Lucknow, of which language and poetry of the land stands out best. Literary critics and historians have explored thousands of great poets, and their influence is obvious in the works of contemporary poets.

Like Mir Taqi Mir influenced Firaq Gorakhpuri and Nasir Kazmi, Sauda touched Faiz Ahmad Faiz, and Aatish mesmerised Yagana Changezi and Shakeel Badayuni. The poetics of all the above names had enchanted Majaz Lakhnavi and Josh Malihabadi, Jameel Mazhari and Ali Sardar Jafri, and so on.

Mehru Jaffer's translations of the poetry of Mir Anees and of others are sure to rekindle interest in the great poets of Lucknow, and that is what makes this anthology so significant.

—Iftikhar Arif
Islamabad, 2022

Introduction

'A river survives if it flows,
but it lives when refreshed by tributaries.'

This Kenyan saying aptly describes the difference between surviving and living. A language is comparable to a river, sometimes gushing down to formulate itself, at others taking detours to overcome obstructions, placid and solemn, to allow space for the expansion of thought, running into whirlpools to churn ideas and philosophy. Any living language is continuously flowing, and its users travel with it to explore its journey, to make their contributions to what might be called their trek but which is essentially the voyage of the language river.

Urdu was initially overlooked as a *rekhta* or mixture, and supposedly considered not suitable for the creation of poetry. It, however, took a very short time for poets, connoisseurs and critics to realise the possibilities that a developing language has to offer. It must have been followed by the realisation that the poetry in this language will have its reach among a huge mass of population. The allure to be understood and appreciated across the country, besides the novelty of exploring the vocabularies of Persian, Arabic, delving into the available proverbs, idioms, symbols and metaphors of so many surrounding dialects, must have been an enticement for anyone occupying themselves with words.

This book begins with a journey, and aptly so, since Urdu is a language that is constantly in travel. Mir Taqi Mir, perhaps the finest of Urdu poets, is leaving Delhi and travelling to Lucknow. He knows that Lucknow is the new patronage centre—rich in its resources but not very promising by way of the contribution of the end product to its benefaction. While Mir's financial condition might have been the immediate reason for his immigration from Delhi to Lucknow, one would also have to think of the opportunity that a rich state and a benevolent ruler willing to support a writer writing in a largely unexplored language would have to offer.

Upheavals and political unrest were routine in Delhi after Aurangzeb, besides the systemic attacks and plunder by outsiders. Even though Urdu had continued to develop in Delhi, exploring the boundaries of verse and creating new forms like *dastangoi*, it was but natural for the language to move eastwards, and instinctive for a poet of Mir's calibre to follow it.

It is difficult to pin down Mir to a category or a type. He was the first of the Urdu poets who questioned everything around him, be it religion, tradition, neglect of the masses, or belief. He also never refrained from expressing his opinion. His couplets are deeply rooted in philosophy, spirituality and Sufism. With that, he is also among the first poets who connected with nature and unashamedly expressed the desire to enjoy its bounties. For all this and more that is found in the poetry of Mir, tranquillity is required.

A strong craving for independence by the nawabs of Lucknow had led to the process of distancing from the Mughal rulers that bordered on a nonviolent form of rebellion. Avadh began coming into its own, generating its own revenue and pocketing it, breaking free from the shackles of Delhi politics and linguistic constraints, thereby allowing it to bestow patronage. This peaceful insurgence adopted by the rulers seeped into the psyche of the inhabitants of Lucknow, steering in experimentation in all forms of life. Cuisine, clothing, music, dance, language and poetry—everything provided space for trials and testing, yielding a novelty of imagination and ingenuity that was quickly absorbed into the cultural structure of the state. The most to benefit from this newfound freedom was Urdu. It is not surprising that the popular slogan for revolution that has travelled to every language of India and resonates in each and every protest comes from Urdu: Inquilab Zindabad! (Long live the revolution!)

Sustenance of the independence in Avadh demanded that new political links be investigated, and the nawabs of Lucknow formed liaisons with local Rajput, Kayastha and Khatri sects. This boosted the development of the economy, made space for the interaction and formation of a strong base with locals, and, most importantly, helped in the development of Urdu.

It is in Lucknow that Urdu opens itself up to the dialects spoken in the surrounding regions of Lucknow. Proverbs, idioms, allusions of the dialects like Avadhi, Purabi and Bhojpuri flowed into Urdu as did the appreciation of *doha* and *chaupai*, the two important forms of expression of Hindi poetry. These interactions also brought with them legends, myths, parables and fables that formed the base for the emergence of Urdu prose.

I recall an incident from my childhood. The ten-year census was in progress and a volunteer was taking down the details of our family from my parents. When he came to 'mother tongue' and inquired whether it was Hindi or Urdu, my father, Sajjad Zaheer, involuntarily said 'Avadhi', and my mother, Razia, spontaneously uttered 'Marwari'. The strong bond and commitment of these two writers to the language could not bypass their love for the dialects that had enriched the river of Urdu. However, knowledge of the Urdu language would not be forsaken in their household.

I was not taught Urdu in school, so learning the script was dutifully taken up at home by my parents. When I was seven, Abba decided that I should be made familiar with Urdu poetry. He laughingly turned 'an apple a day keeps the doctor away' to 'a sher a day keeps the blues away', and I learnt an Urdu couplet in the morning to recite in the evening. Not to be left out, Ammi coined, 'a story a night keeps nightmares away', and bedtime was devoted to stories from the Panchatantra, Ramayana and Mahabharata, riddles and homophones from the writings of Amir Khusrau, and dohas and *savaiyas* from Kabir, Rahim and Raskhan. They remain my most fulfilling memories of childhood and fruitful education.

As Lucknow grew and Urdu developed, it was no longer just a literary activity—it became a way of life. It was a tool to learn good manners, an instrument to practise etiquette, a device to indulge in spirituality and a weapon to cut the rival to the core. It was not all fun and games. The literature that was produced demanded knowledge of several languages, flavours of the dialects, constant practice and serious exchange with contemporaries.

This fundamental requirement of the language to be able to flourish was acknowledged by the well-to-do of the city who willingly became patrons of gatherings of poets, writers and linguists. Termed as *mehfils* and *mushairas*, these assemblies became the churning pots of poetry and literature. From the beggar in the street to the courtesan, from the chefs, the shopkeepers and the roadside vendors to the street singers and eunuchs, all complemented the city's rulers and their love for aesthetics in dance, music, repartee on themes of mourning, love, etc., cuisine and even perfumes. The people of Lucknow loved all that the city was giving them. Life in Lucknow was not just lived, it was celebrated.

It was in Lucknow that Urdu, borrowing the style and manner of expression of Persian, integrating the many dialects of the milieu, matured as a local language with the strength to lend itself equally to classical as well as folk literature. Schools flourished where debates over language—its lyricism, purity and the liberties that one could take with it—were a full-time occupation. Poetry became the expression of love, heartache, spirituality and rivalry, and also of humour and satire. Some poets used and refined satire and innuendos, while others indulged in it.

The language which blossomed in Lucknow bred cultural integration across religion, caste, class and gender. In a very short span of time, Urdu developed a freedom of expression that is found only in the free-flowing language of the masses. Lucknow became the melting pot that valued spirituality as much as sensuality.

Perhaps the most insightful example of the amalgam of the physical with the mystical is the evolution of the performing arts. Kathak, Thumri, Dadra, Chaiti and, most specifically, Qawwali, which had been in existence since Amir Khusrau, now came into their own in Lucknow.

Within a very short span of time, the relationship of the language with its practitioners transformed. Language from being a means of communication turned into a form of expression. Poets indulged the philosophies, lovingly nurturing and making demands of it to rise to their expectations and be the muse that would inspire their thoughts, ideas, philosophies and beliefs. This exchange between the muse and the creator generated an atmosphere of round-the-clock festivity. Citizens of the state took to this revelry as a duck takes to water. In the process, the approach of language to emotion went through a metamorphosis.

One of the masters of this transformation of language into an experience was Mir Anees. With a single incident of Karbala and the martyrdom of Hazrat Husain and his family, Anees created a panorama that pictured the entire navarasa of the Natyashastra. Using Karbala, Anees developed the aesthetics of mourning. This was echoed by other important poets like Dabir and many Hindu poets. *Marsiya* or elegy had been missing from Indian literature. Ancient epics contained several incidents of martyrdom, yet they had not dwelled on death as an important part of life nor had they extolled it as a conscious decision that has to be mourned. Anees visualised the martyrdom of seventy-two male members of Hazrat Husain's family, juxtaposing it with current politics, social set-up, ongoing rivalries and contemporary dogmas. In the process,

Anees liberated Hazrat Husain from the confines of a single religion and gave the incident of Karbala a universality. The popularity of Muharram and the celebration of accepting death for a cause gave Lucknow its plural society where Hindu poets contributed with their poetry in participating in the ten-day mourning for the martyrdom and rejoicing at the survival of the cause. Anees, in his exploration, freed Karbala from the confines of faith. He delved deep into his chosen subject and transformed Husain from an individual into an ideology that would always symbolise truth and justice.

Anees was able to gain this acceptance, followed by fame that has survived over two centuries, through the use of everyday speech in poetry. His verses are so simple in style and idioms that it is almost prose, that anyone reading it would feel that they too can write it. But it is the ease with which marsiya flows that makes it so difficult to replicate. Pampered and cajoled by poets, musicians, dancers, theatre persons, so exuberant had become the culture, so deep-rooted the practice of the aesthetics that even when the state of Avadh was swallowed by the East India Company, and its ruler Wajid Ali Shah left Lucknow for Calcutta, the tradition of sophistication survived and remained the identity of the city.

It is here and in Urdu that for the first time the female voice is explored. Attributed to Rangini for its development, it stood on the side of the women, exploring the emotions of the female in a relationship and creating space to express lovemaking as enjoyable and earthly for women too. Not popular at the time of its inception, it was soon dropped from the bubbling pot of Urdu literature. It remained as a shut door—but one that could be opened.

It is impossible to think of colonialism and not mention the role of Lucknow and its cultural ethos in the freedom movement. The siege of the Lucknow Residency that lasted for nine months happened after the last nawab of Lucknow had left the city. It is the first and the only example in the history of the struggle for Independence of the people's resistance to save what belonged to them. The battle was not between the ousted rulers and the vanquisher. It was a confrontation of a refined culture rejecting the usurper. Defeated after a nine-month-long blockade, this resistance survived in the collective memory of the people. Innumerable folk songs, even thumri and nautanki, were written about the occurrence. Music, dance, theatre and poetry became tools to hand down legends as reminiscences to the future generations. This was the way of a thriving culture to counter colonialism and its cultural onslaught.

Somewhere in the middle of the nineteenth century, the physical had taken over from the spiritual world. In Lucknow, it began with poets and thinkers exploring sensuality that bordered on the erotic. But perhaps it was this physicality that broadened itself in the minds of the poets of the early twentieth century and set the stage for the formation of the Progressive Writers' Association (PWA).

The arrival of the first letter press had already made literature available to everyone. Reading had become a source of not only a good job but also of enjoyment and entertainment. It was in keeping with the culture and tradition that the PWA should have begun from the city of Lucknow to shed a new light, new approach, new role and different kind of appreciation of literature. It is only right that a city that had allowed the inclusion of the common people into the development of its culture should now cater to their demand that their conditions be mirrored in contemporary poetry, become the spine of modern fiction, and construct a system of criticism that would change the aesthetic value.

The first conference of the PWA was held in Lucknow on 9–10 April 1936 at the Rafa-e-Aam Club. It was presided over by the great Urdu writer Munshi Premchand who said in his presidential address that the Progressives would have to change the ethics of aesthetics. When this conscious change happens in the mind of the beholder, beauty will be found in the tired limbs of the working-class labourer. Then poets and writers shall write about the masses and shall be the voice that would call out the injustice being meted out to the exploited masses. The tenets of progressive writing would spread from Urdu and Lucknow to all the languages of India, ushering in a directness and starkness in the handling of issues like poverty, hunger, exploitation and inequality. The movement of progressive writing did spread all over the country, and soon every song written and sung for the freedom of the country, every slogan raised against colonialism, and every call given for the overthrow of imperialism had its roots in a progressive pen.

With progressive ideology travelled the influence of the Urdu language and poetry. In the last decade or so, I have come across writers of other languages imbibing the formats of metre and verse of Urdu into their own language of expression. It is not surprising to come across a ghazal in Marathi, Gujarati, or Tamil contemporary poetry. The most recent addition has been ghazals in Sanskrit. When a much-loved form, nurtured with care and adoration by the practitioners of one language, confined to a region, breaks boundaries and finds a home in another language in another geographical corner, it is for all practical purposes an acclamation of both the primary language and the initial culture.

It is an ethos that will change form and modify itself, allowing new tributaries to make their contribution. This shall keep the river flowing and the language shall never die.

—Noor Zaheer
London, June 2023

In Love With Words in Lucknow

With Braj on one side and Ayodhya, Prayagraj and Kashi on the other, the region of Avadh is blessed with thinkers, philosophers, saints and poets spouting words of beauty and wisdom since ancient times. The study of the Vedas accompanied by enlightened discourses has been a tradition that laid a foundation for *shastrath* or scholarly interaction from an early age in the Indo-Gangetic plains. Inheriting traditions of Bhakti poets of *nirgun* (invisible) and *sargun* (visible) streams providing examples of popular colloquial communication, Avadh developed a space for socio-religious and cultural cross-pollination for subsequent generations of poets and writers to follow. Sufi poet Maulana Dawood chose the folklore of Lorik and Chanda to write *Chandayan*, the first *khadi boli* (local dialect) Sufi love poem, in 1389.

A practising Muslim, Malik Muhammad Jayasi from near Amethi in the Avadh region, schooled in the philosophy of Vedanta and Kabir's couplets, wrote a *masnavi* (a long poem in rhyming couplets) *Padmavat* in 1540. Alauddin Khilji's pursuit of Rani Padmini is the subject of this epic from the geographical area of Chittor, Rajasthan, written in the village of Avadh. Besides these individual efforts, a major institution of learning took root in Lucknow when the Firangi Mahal seminary got established to study mathematics, astronomy and philosophy along with the study of the Quran in the seventeenth century, enhancing its charming cosmopolitan character. By the late eighteenth century, Avadh, being a fertile prosperous area, was quite insulated from attacks by a treaty with the East India Company, unlike the Mughal capital Delhi that was subjected to looting and plundering by forces emboldened by a regime on the decline. Much like the political equation where the weakening of a single party rule gives way to coalition of sorts, the Persian language in the court of the Mughal dynasty saw the cobbling together of a language of the masses called Rekhta, with words from several Indian, Persian and Arabic sources. What initially began as a link language between soldiers of various linguistic backgrounds in the Mughal cavalry very close to the Jama Masjid area of today soon became a symbol of native aspirations and identity with extensive everyday use. From a collection of a smattering of dialects of khadi boli, an entire language was born with an original syntax and grammar that fired up the world with its universal content. With the migration of a large section of soldiers and traders with the Burhan-ul-Mulk from Delhi to Avadh, Rekhta and Urdu also found a second home after Delhi. Lucknow and its surroundings adapted it as a refined version of local dialects suitable for an inter-class communication cutting across social hierarchy.

Poetry in Rekhta, unlike most other languages, began with non-religious subjects. It had an anti-fundamental, liberal streak in its demeanour right from the beginning. The regular plundering of Delhi by Rohillas and Marathas and Ahmad Shah Abdali's sack of Delhi each year starting 1748 as well as the recurring insecurities made several scholars and poets like Arzoo, Sauda and Mir move to Lucknow at the court of Asaf-ud-Daula—a choice forced by circumstances. The Delhi that Mir had seen and had left behind could never leave him. Distressed to witness the plundering of his beloved city, he gave vent to his feelings through some of his couplets:

Udti hai khaak sheher ki galiyon mein ab jahaan
Sona liya hai goad mein bhar kar wahin se hum

Where dust drifts in the alleys of the city now
I had my lap filled with gold in earlier days.

Mir Taqi Mir brought in a delightful synthesis of Persian and North Indian khadi boli traditions with Prakrit figures of speech in what then was still called Rekhta. Mirza Ghalib once said with envy for Mir:

Rekhte ke tum hi ustad nahi ho 'Ghalib'
Kehte hain agle zamaane mein koi 'Mir' bhi thha

You are not the only master of Rekhta, O 'Ghalib'
There was someone named 'Mir' before you.

When ghazals were still composed and couplets were said and not written, Ustad Khan Arzoo can be attributed with laying the foundation of Urdu poetry in Avadh in the 1740s. Ghazals had a major role in nursing the language in the early Rekhta days, helping it blossom as Urdu by expanding the horizon with their diction and range with other forms like *qasida* (an ode or poetic tribute) and *rubai* (verses of four lines).

The important phase of the Lucknow school of Urdu poetry was driven largely by the disciples of Khan Arzoo who were all immigrants to the city. Poets like Mirza Jaafar Ali 'Hasrat', Mir Haider Ali 'Hairaan', Khwaja Hasan 'Hasan', Mirza Faakhar 'Haseen' made Lucknow their home. The poems written by these poets in the new language acquired popular and public appeal in no time.

Known as *Khuda-e-Sukhan*, Mir Taqi Mir can be credited with settling the template of Urdu ghazal and masnavi by 1800. Using an intimate and informal tone with *Tu*, *Tum*, *Unne*, *Pyaare*, *Sahib* very often as a form of address in his poems, Mir understood the importance of connecting with a listener in verbal communication, and his poems most of the time take the form of a vocal address with an interesting phonetic, aural structure. And like the saint poets of an earlier era, he never lost sight of being accessible to the layman:

Sher mere hain sab khaas pasand
Par mujhe guftugu awaam se hai

My couplets are liked by the elite
But I converse with the masses.

It is difficult to separate Lucknow from the identity of anyone who has lived there even for a few years. Citizens of Lucknow even today live in twin cities of nostalgia of the erstwhile and the contemporary Lucknow. The Lucknow of Wajid Ali Shah as described by Ruswa (author of *Umrao Jaan*), Sarshar and Majaaz remains a sub-conscious force to the Lucknow that has been shaped with the reign of Mayavati, Akhilesh and Yogi ji today.

Mehru Jaffer has painstakingly researched the evolution of Urdu poetry and how it chose Lucknow as a refuge and its massive social spread. This book is bound to create further interest in the subsequent form and shape this legacy acquired in the Lucknow of twentieth century that was inherited and taken forward by the likes of Ratan Nath Sarshar, Brij Narayan Chakbast, Hasrat Mohani, Ramprasad Bismil, Kavi Pradeep, Arzoo Lucknawi by Josh Malihabadi, Amritlal Nagar, Bhagwati Charan Verma, Yashpal, Majaaz, Kunwar Narain and Raghuveer Sahay who looked at the very established norm with a new sensibility.

—Salim Arif
Mumbai, April 2023

ONE

Mir Sahab on the Road

The colourful caravan of the tinker, tailor, soldier, sailor, spy, pimp and prostitute snaking its way from Delhi to Lucknow had included Urdu poet Mir Muhammad Taqi Mir. The *Khuda-e-Sukhan*, a wizard with words, was silent for a change amidst the hustle and bustle created by those migrating with him to Lucknow. Mir was sulking because he had to leave Delhi to make a home in Lucknow. Already recognised as the finest lyrical poet of classical Urdu, Mir was travelling to Lucknow on a personal invitation from Nawab Asaf-ud-Daula, the ruler of the north Indian province of Avadh. However, Mir had packed his bags reluctantly. The thought that he could not live in Delhi anymore made Mir sad and angry.

When Asaf-ud-Daula heard that the sixty-year-old poet was without an income in Delhi, he had invited Mir to Lucknow as court luminary. Mir liked the idea of being wealthy. He looked forward to the security that he was promised in Lucknow, but he was contemptuous of the poetry that was being written in the city. The verses sounded effete and artificial to him. He found no sincerity, no depth of feeling, no flame of lament, no tone of longing in poetry that was being written in Avadh. In Lucknow, poets had stripped love of its spiritual content and substituted it with verbal jugglery. Poetry in Lucknow was all about praise for the physical beauty of the beloved without any interest in the spiritual depth of the loved one.

He recalled two lines by Asaf-ud-Daula himself and cringed. Asaf-ud-Daula wrote that the manner in which he was greeted by his beloved made him captive in a moment:

Iss adaa se mujhe salaam kiya
Ek hi aan mein ghulaam kiya

Mir was a self-confessed *ghampasand*, a mate of misery, a groom of grief and a lover of loneliness. He was concerned about his presence amidst superficial gaiety and the reported lack of lofty interests in Lucknow. He had heard stories about the river of wealth that flowed through the city and about the proliferation of pleasure amongst the people. Poetry was used in Lucknow for coquetry and to express people's infatuation with feminine beauty, often in coarse language. He was excited at the thought of a regular income and looked forward to being at the centre of political and cultural activities that the boomtown saw under the patronage of Asaf-ud-Daula. But how did the austere and dignified poet from the venerable but decaying Mughal city plan to cope with life in the frivolous new centre of wealth and patronage?

All those poets who had migrated from Delhi before him sounded less sincere to Mir in Lucknow. Syed Muhammad Mir Soz wrote that death is inevitable, but if it occurs with the head on her lap then it is a dream come true:

Sar zaanu pe ho usske aur jaan nikal jaaye
Marna toh musallam hai armaan nikal jaaye

It is true that life in Lucknow was promiscuous. It was sensual, but it was also gentle in comparison to Delhi. People were carefree and pleasure-loving. Mir was told that the society in Lucknow was excessively colourful and extravagant, that conversation amongst citizens was contrived, like their laughter. Casual innuendo and exaggerated introductions were in plenty but were forgotten within minutes. There were lots of effusive meetings between people, even when no one was aware of the name of the other.

Mir was a traditional man. He was proud, sensitive and glum by temperament. He wrote the most heartfelt lyrics about love that people admired, but many of his admirers regretted his arrogance. As his journey neared Lucknow, Mir's gloom magnified and he experienced a sense of unease. He wondered if he had made the right decision to move to Lucknow. He wished to find refuge in a more civilised place than the licentious capital of Asaf-ud-Daula.

Once in Lucknow, he found the city gloomy and difficult to live in. He felt that its streets stank like an Abyssinian's armpits. Despite the aversion, Mir lived in Lucknow for twenty-eight years and is buried here. Throughout his stay, Mir spent a lot of that time alone and with memories of Delhi. He longed for the city he had left behind. For Mir, one ruined Delhi was worth ten (remarkable) Lucknows. He raised many an eyebrow when he said that he should have died in Delhi and not come to Lucknow to weep. People in Lucknow found Mir a difficult man, ill-tempered and ungrateful to a city that gave him refuge and a dream job as court poet in the fairyland-like fiefdom of Asaf-ud-Daula.

For nearly a decade Mir had no regular income. He was not doing much in Delhi when he received a letter from Asaf-ud-Daula. In *Zikr-i-Mir*, his autobiography originally in Persian, the poet writes, 'I was sitting at home disgusted with life when I read the letter. I immediately set out for Lucknow.'

Mir had accepted Asaf-ud-Daula's invite out of necessity, but he did not look forward to attending court in Lucknow as he hated the idea of being a courtier. The thought of dancing attendance on aristocracy embarrassed him. Yet Mir needed to earn money. In Delhi he was on the verge of starvation and had desperately looked for employment when all that Delhi had to offer its citizens at that time was blood and gore. The city was overrun by robbers and murderers, and beggars and kings tried to grab as much as they could. The poor were more at peace because thieves had left them alone. Those were the days when poverty was the only wealth worth enjoying in Delhi.

The old Mughal Delhi had been destroyed and its citizens had dispersed, including its poets. Political unrest and violence were routine after the death of Aurangzeb, the last of the great Mughal rulers, in 1707. Aurangzeb had left his sons to follow the dreadful tradition of succession that was often filled with bloodshed. That weakened the Mughal administration and the army. Former subjects in different parts of the country had taken up arms against the vast Mughal empire and there were serious threats from outsiders as well. The post-Mughal states were based on ethnic or sectarian groups like Marathas, Jats and Sikhs. The Marathas dreamt of inheriting the Mughal throne and so did the Bundelas, Rajputs and the Sikhs.

Mir was barely twelve years old when he left Agra, his place of birth, to live in Delhi. Muhammad Shah Rangeela was the Mughal emperor. He was a useless administrator but a fine patron of music and the arts. It is during his reign that Maharaja Jai Singh II of Jaipur was inspired to build the Jantar Mantar observatory. It remains a landmark in Delhi and is still used to calculate eclipses of the sun and moon, and the movement of stars. Muhammad Shah came to the throne at a time when the Mughal empire was shrunk within the boundary of Delhi. It was not the emperor but the nobility that held the reign of power. Muhammad Shah was disinterested in politics, but he was a lover of poetry and of female beauty and had little clue as to how he could check the disintegration of his empire. His indifferent reign coincided with hordes of warriors who pushed open the north-western passes in the mountain to barge into India. The Mughal army tried to drive the intruders back, but it was defeated.

Led by Emperor Nadir Shah, Persian soldiers seized the moment as a golden opportunity to rob the militarily weak but wealthy city of Delhi. The attack on Delhi by Nadir Shah, and later Ahmad Shah Abdali, the Afghan, combined with the suicidal internal feuds of the Mughal nobility destroyed the Mughal empire. By 1761, Delhi was left to fend for itself.

Persian soldiers had marched into South Asia, looting towns on their way to Delhi. Ordinary citizens tried to resist the intruders. As Nadir Shah entered Delhi, people pelted stones at him and a shot was fired that killed a Persian soldier. Nadir Shah was furious at the death of his soldier. He hurried up to the rooftop of a mosque and menacingly stood between the domes shimmering in gold. From that height he surveyed the Chandni Chowk neighbourhood lying at his feet, waved his sword and ordered a massacre. No one was to be left alive in any part of Delhi where his men were killed, he said. That day in March 1739, Nadir Shah killed 20,000–1,50,000 people before he turned his back on Delhi.

Mir was just a teenager when the Persian warrior Nadir Shah had attacked Delhi. He had witnessed members of the royal family trooping out of the fort and begging for alms. For the rest of his life, he was haunted by scenes of attack that forced Mughal princesses to sleep in hovels and thousands to queue up every day for a free meal at a local house of prayer. After stealing Mughal Emperor Shah Jahan's peacock throne and the Kohinoor diamond from the Red Fort, Nadir Shah had returned to Persia. A few years later, when Nadir Shah's Afghan general Ahmad Shah Abdali returned to attack and loot, he had a free run as there was no one to guard Delhi. Abdali pulled out precious stones from the palace walls and killed without mercy anyone who crossed his path. Nadir Shah and Abdali wreaked such havoc in Delhi that after their loot the Mughals were unable to retain their power as an all-India empire.

Mir witnessed the plunder of Delhi by Abdali and he wrote:

> The Afghans and Rohilla Pathans started their work of slaughter and plunder, breaking down doors, tying up those they found inside and in many cases burning them alive or cutting off their heads. Everywhere was bloodshed and destruction and for three days and nights this savagery continued … men who had been pillars

> of the state were brought to nothing, men of noble rank left destitute, family men bereft of all their loved ones. Most of them roamed the streets amid insult and humiliation. Wives and children were made captive and the killing and looting went on unchecked.

How was anyone supposed to be happy under the circumstances? The safety and security of the old world of luxury was ruined. People no longer sauntered in and out of each other's life. Hearts had shrunk out of fear of one human being, for another. The regular meet and greet between citizens had come to a standstill. The streets crawled not with storytellers and hawkers selling goods, but with thieves and killers. There was no one left to pour wine to the poet anymore. The tea houses and taverns were pulled down. Laughter was rare and the cry of distressed citizens from dawn to dusk was unbearable as it bounced back and forth around the city from one wall to another.

The only good that came out of all the cruelty around Mir was poignancy that crept into his heart and mind, making his poetry so profound. Here Mir says that the whole world, including every leaf in the garden of life and every bud, is aware of the poet's malaise, except for the rose:

Patta patta boota boota haal humaara jaane hai
Jaane na jaane gul hi na jaane baagh toh saara jaane hai

Mir had no choice but to leave a distressed Delhi behind. Part of the luggage that accompanied him to Lucknow was a bundle of papers and bags full of grief.

Mir grieved because he felt he could not live anywhere except in Delhi anymore. He fell prey to bouts of melancholia at the thought that he would never again recline on the steps of the city's majestic Jama Masjid and watch the world go by. He was already missing the heat and dust of the streets of Shahjahanabad and the sound and fury of Delhi's Jama Masjid neighbourhood where Mir spent a great deal of his time. He remembered the generosity of street vendors who competed with each other in serving him a plate of finger-licking lunch in return for a verse recited by the poet. The cobbler was happy to mend Mir's shoes for the same price and the tailor made sure that the tear in Mir's attire was not visible. Remembering his street friends made Mir smile, but memories of hungry princesses wailing inside Delhi's Red Fort made his nose bleed.

In contrast, Avadh was well-to-do and tranquil. The Lucknow that Mir had travelled to in 1782 was groomed by Asaf-ud-Daula into a world-class cultural capital, where the skyline competed with the breathtakingly beautiful silhouette of Constantinople.

It was Mughal Emperor Akbar who chose to develop Lucknow as a commercial hub in the sixteenth century. In 1722, Faizabad was the capital of Burhan-ul-Mulk Saadat Ali Khan, founder of the Lucknow dynasty of rulers and the great grandfather of Asaf-ud-Daula. Faizabad was founded 20 km away from Ayodhya, the sacred capital of the Suryavanshi rulers of the area of whom Rama is the most famous.

Saadat Ali Khan was a Shia Muslim immigrant from Persia. He was appointed a military official in the Mughal army and sent by the Mughal emperor to Avadh to arm-twist local landlords to pay their dues to Delhi. The landlords in the region had armed themselves against each other and tried to grab more power and hold on to as much arable land as possible. Saadat Ali Khan was successful in overpowering the rebellious landlords and seizing Lucknow from them. He had squashed dissent against Delhi's Mughal ruler and disciplined rebels. He put together a well-paid, well-armed, well-trained army and made alliances with all the rivals of the dissenting landlords. As reward, the province of Avadh was gifted by the Mughal emperor to Saadat Ali Khan.

The Persian courtier was first and foremost a warrior, and spent more time on the battlefield than in any palace. Whenever he visited Avadh, he had lived in a temporary tent-city, surrounded by mud houses in Faizabad. His main concern was to make sure that all revenue owed to the Mughal emperor was collected. Saadat Khan did not intimidate the ordinary population of the area. He fought only the rebellious landlords and touched base with the local people. To make himself feel at home, he looked into the grievances of different groups of people, adopting an open and non-combative relationship with the population of the territory which he had successfully conquered.

Along with Muslim *shaikhzadas*, he reached out to the Rajput community. Hindus from the Kayastha and Khatri communities were given important positions in the administration. He tried to integrate the aspirations of upper-caste Rajputs with those of the Muslim elite. He reached out to non-Rajput Hindu urban elites as well and succeeded in achieving a political balance in the region. He avoided conflicts and encouraged integration and assimilation, inspiring his successors to administer Avadh in the same way.

His successor Safdarjung continued to serve the Mughal emperor and lived mostly in Delhi. Safdarjung's son and successor Shuja-ud-Daula made Faizabad his capital in 1765 and made the province accessible to foreigners. He employed French mercenaries in his court. The British painter Tilly Kettle lived in Faizabad and produced many a portrait of the rulers of Avadh.

Shuja-ud-Daula got Mirza Muhammad Rafi Sauda, the Delhi-born master of elegies and satire, to teach him to write poetry. Asaf-ud-Daula was Shuja-ud-Daula's son, successor, poet and a great builder. He was a practising Shia Muslim and dotted the city with magnificent buildings that were populated with artists, learned people and poets, including Sauda who held a special place at his court. Syed Muhammad Mir Soz had followed Sauda to Lucknow in 1778 and he was Asaf-ud-Daula's mentor in composing verse. The love poems of Asaf-ud-Daula are surely inspired by Soz as he addresses the rose to say that the flower is dear to him because it has the same perfume as the beloved:

Aye gul tujhe azeez hoon rakhta main isliye
Yaani ki tujh mein ek ramaq bu-e-yaar hai

Sauda was a decade older than Mir and he died a year before Mir came to live in Lucknow in 1782. But Mir remembered Sauda in Delhi as a young man who was cheerful and wrote extremely well.

Here Sauda makes his reader smile as he claims that his poetry recitations in the garden make nightingales (bulbul, koel and cuckoo are birds from the same family; both bulbul and koel are indigenous to India) go crazy.

Karun chaman mein agar jaake main ghazal khvaani
Toh bulbulein hoyen mere chehchahaane ki deewani

Sauda's satires are superb and he never let go of his wit even amidst the unfortunate circumstances that encompassed him. In this couplet, Sauda says that he is not aware of what love is, but his heart feels like it is in the embrace of a flame.

Ishq se toh nahin hoon main vaaqif
Dil ko shola sa kuchh lipat-ta hai

Before his death in 1739, Saadat Ali Khan had made the job of the provincial head appointed to Avadh by the Mughal emperor a hereditary position. This was the first brick laid to the foundation of the Lucknow dynasty. Now the position of the nawab of Avadh was upgraded to an independent ruler with a personal fiefdom. The word nawab is a corruption of the Persian word *naib*, or viceroy. Saadat Ali Khan's successors Nawab Safdarjung, Nawab Shuja-ud-Daula and Nawab Asaf-ud-Daula were politically astute and provided stability in Avadh. They found freedom in Lucknow to practise rites and rituals in imitation of the traditions of Shia Muslims of Iran. Especially during Muharram, Lucknow lit up as a capital city of Shia traditions that flowed out on to the street as an invitation for all citizens irrespective of the religion they followed to join in. Muharram is the first month of the Islamic calendar when Husain, one of the two grandsons of Muhammad, the Prophet of Islam, was martyred by a cruel dictator in the seventh century.

Asaf-ud-Daula was a practising Shia, but he did not break away from the Sunni Muslim Mughal emperor. Artfully, he had distanced himself from the domination of Delhi, but he continued to be polite and courteous in public to family members of the Mughals. Never abusing etiquette, he hosted many Timurid princes in Lucknow, including Mirza Sulaiman Shikoh, Mirza Ilahi Baksh and Mirza Husain Baksh who had fled Delhi. All of them were treated with grace at the all-too-polite high culture practised at the court of Asaf-ud-Daula.

Asaf-ud-Daula was generous and always made it a point to stand up from his throne at the arrival of a Mughal prince, and to make him sit next to him. Asaf-ud-Daula did so even when he was unwell and in pain after a fall from a horse once. However, in his enthusiasm to be independent of Delhi, he did make the mistake of confiding too much in the officials of the British East India Company. Asaf-ud-Daula failed to realise in time how the British had increased their interference in the day-to-day affairs of his kingdom and he believed the Company when its officials promised to stand by him and his throne like a rock. He built the Residency, a luxurious riverside residence, for the British East India Company representative in Lucknow at an immense cost. The Company took advantage of Asaf-ud-Daula's generosity and continued to fleece Avadh to finance its wars in Bengal, South India and with the Marathas. The Company representative in Lucknow was called the Resident, and his sole job was to trick the wealthy rulers of Avadh to provide the Company with financial support. Company officials spent much of their time in Avadh extorting money from wherever they could, including from the wealthy grandmother and mother of Asaf-ud-Daula in Faizabad. Fed up of being caught between the political games played by the British within his family, Asaf-ud-

Daula left Faizabad to make a home in Lucknow. The British naturally followed Asaf-ud-Daula to Lucknow and, over time, the Residency became a parallel and, later, dominant centre of power. It was at the Residency that Company officials plotted and planned the eventual colonisation of Avadh.

There was no dearth of money in Avadh as it flowed into Lucknow from the rich agricultural produce in the heartland of the province. Avadh remained comparatively peaceful during the rule of Asaf-ud-Daula and matters of security were handled by the British in a bid to buy peace.

This is the reason why all roads led to Lucknow when most parts of the country had rocked with social and political unrest. Under the rulers of Avadh, the city had replaced Delhi as a centre of high culture. The Lucknow dynasty continued the tradition of patronage to cultural activities in the footsteps of the Slave Dynasty of the Sultans of Delhi and later the Mughals. The end of the eighteenth century saw a huge wave of immigrants who had arrived in search of employment in Lucknow.

Lucknow came alive as a hub of hectic activity involving Urdu literature, and welcomed talent from around the world. Company officials, including European traders living in Lucknow, were part of the wealthy political elite. All of them played games of self-interest with each other. What united this motley group of people with different interests was their common love for the Urdu language. It was not confined to any one religious or ethnic community but was a heritage of the entire population. The Urdu language was the glue that brought together a secular community of people who met each other regularly to recite poetry under the stars and sometimes inside a delicately carved *baradari* in marble. Poetry recitations took place in the marketplace and on the steps of a church, a temple and a mosque. Poets also jammed on boats on the River Gomti gilded in gold and silver and carved in the shape of a fish. There was poetry to be enjoyed in the company of a courtesan under the trembling wick of an oil lamp. In the Lucknow of Asaf-ud-Daula, Urdu poetry was not just a literary activity—it was life.

In *The Raj, the Indian Mutiny and the Kingdom of Oudh, 1801–1859*, author John Pemble writes:

> After the decline of Delhi, only in Lucknow was that tradition of courtly opulence maintained that had made India envy of the world. The lifestyle of Asaf-ud-Daula, ruler of Lucknow at the turn of the eighteenth century, was the most opulent and unthinkable anywhere else in India at the time. The wealth and security of Lucknow exercised a powerful attraction on the poets, musicians, scholars and professional men who had till recently subsisted on the bounty of the Mughal court. When Delhi could no longer support them, they made their way almost en masse to Lucknow which soon became the centre of the most urbane, literate and brilliant society in India. Lucknow was thus the inheritor of the role once filled by Delhi as the focus of high culture learning and fashion in the subcontinent.

The Firangi Mahal seminary had already established Lucknow's reputation as a city of learning in the seventeenth century. The seminary was well known for its scientific syllabus. People came from around the world to study mathematics, astronomy and philosophy along with the study of the Quran. There were students from Bukhara, Heart, Kabul, Cairo and Damascus at the Firangi Mahal, giving the city a charming cosmopolitan character.

The rulers of Lucknow built splendid libraries and spent time learning to compose verse. They enjoyed music as much as matters of the military. The royal taste for poetry affected the entire society. Literary symposiums or *mushairas* were routine in which a great number of citizens participated. Mushairas were held both privately and in public places. Lucknow in the nineteenth century had developed into something of a Parnassus, the limestone mountain in central Greece above Delphi, mythical home of many a muse and haven of poetry, music and learning.

In the attractive ambience of Lucknow, the Urdu language blossomed more beautifully than a rose in paradise. The language matured into a graceful lingua franca decked in vocabulary borrowed from the local dialects of Avadhi and Brajbhasha. In the eighteenth century, Urdu was an accepted literary language in Delhi, but Persian was the court language. Most well-known poets were judged and applauded for the verses they wrote in Persian. By the time Urdu arrived in Lucknow towards the end of the eighteenth century, it was ready to be crowned the language of the court. In Avadh, Urdu was allowed to thrive free of Sanskrit or Persian anxiety and poets wrote verses that made people feel as if their heart was being scratched by a fingernail.

The language had evolved gradually over centuries from early conversations between Persian-speaking traders, Turkic soldiers, the local population of South Asia and Hindu wives of

Muslim rulers. By the eighteenth century, the language mirrored an extraordinary society of people who had accumulated a wealth of human experiences and shared stories with each other about everything and nothing. Songs, secrets, dreams, favourite foods, language and attire were exchanged along with currency. The literati were paid by wealthy citizens to further nurse and strengthen the language and to formalise its grammar. There came a time when the Urdu language was ready to conquer the world. Unfortunately, by the time that happened, Delhi had lost the prestige it had enjoyed for more than five hundred years. Poetry was still written in Delhi, also in Urdu, but in the midst of insecurity and pain. It was mainly about the sun setting and clouds of sorrow visiting, but seldom departing.

Syed Khwaja Mir Dard, who refused to leave Delhi despite the devastation around him, died in the city of his birth in 1785. In a couplet, Dard wonders if his life is a cyclone as the poet feels thrashed to death by his own stormy hands:

Zindagi hai ya koi toofaan hai
Hum toh iss jeene ke haathon mar chale

To the east of Delhi in Lucknow, Urdu poetry crackled with laughter. Except for the patriarch Saadat Ali Khan and his son-in-law Safdarjung, who were both born in Iran's Nishapur, the succeeding rulers belonging to the Lucknow dynasty were all born in Avadh and the local dialect was their mother tongue. The Persian language that they had learnt from tutors was laced with vocabulary borrowed from Avadhi.

Asaf-ud-Daula expresses his feelings in a couplet that is stripped of Persian as he assures the creator of the world of his devotion, and pleads, using an Avadhi word (*kijjo*), with the ultimate power not to shower so much sorrow upon him:

Yeh 'Asaf' tumhara hai ae banda-parvar
Isse har ghadi tum na dil-gïir kijjo

Delhi had dragged Urdu poetry into gloom. Poets moaned about the temporary nature of worldly joy, the brutal attitude of fate and many took refuge in religion and mysticism. In Lucknow, however, the mood was filled with gaiety. The Urdu language flowered in an atmosphere far more pleasant than in Delhi. The verses written here were full of laughter and tease. Lucknow was the new Mecca of opportunities not only for scholars and poets but also for musicians, book binders, merchants, traders, noblemen, manufacturers, painters and the courtesans. Women from other cities, from the suburbs and from the countryside came to peddle their trade in Lucknow.

The never-ending caravan of courtesans was the most glamourous community of immigrants to arrive here. The women added colourful cadence to life in Lucknow. In the late eighteenth century, *tawaifbazi* or the act of consorting with courtesans became a favourite pastime of the rich and the poor alike. Accompanied by many musical instruments and a rich repertoire of song, dance and poetry, courtesans set up alluring *kotha*s or living quarters on the first floors of shops that lined the lanes of Chowk, Lucknow's main marketplace. Regular visitors to the market made it a habit to look up at the heavens when in the neighbourhood, in the hope of catching even a glimpse of the angel-like creatures often reclining on balconies above. Some of those below on the street were often shy. They were afraid of the thoughts that played on the mind but they could not help themselves from wanting to experience the intoxication that comes from listening to the courtesan speak even a few words.

The courtesans practised an etiquette that attracted citizens to her like the proverbial moth to flame, moths that prefer to singe away their life in order to get closer to the object of love. The courtesans had many ways of alluring admirers. Their knowledge of Urdu poetry and classical Hindustani music was thorough, and they captivated their clients with enchanting dance moves and sensual love songs.

The courtesan of Lucknow was no ordinary being. They were not common prostitutes or fallen women but were highly respected in society. These jewels of the kingdom were rumoured to possess powers that make the mysterious relationship between woman and man even more mystifying. That is why visitors liked to linger in their company to also enjoy an immaculate rendition of seasonal genres like the kajri, saawan, hori and dadra. The thumri, a local Avadhi style, was a favourite even then as it could express extreme love and echo pathos with a passion not possible in any other way of singing.

Many of the courtesans were an alluring bouquet of talent and physical charm, some like sunshine on a winter afternoon. Most of them groomed themselves like a flower in bloom, or mirrored a poet's dream. If one seemed like a full-moon night bathed in the perfume of jasmine blossoms, another resembled a flame flickering at the feet of an idol in a temple. Others were similar to a piece of scorching coal that turns sandalwood slowly into ash, and the proximity of a few felt like sweet talk on the same pillow. Those who came looking for the experience of a lifetime found one quiver like a whiff of breeze just before the crack of dawn, and the next moment ripple like a wave at high tide. Much of the credit of having turned even roadside Romeos into poets goes to the courtesans of Lucknow. It was a ritual for citizens to visit the old Chowk Bazaar area in the evening. At that hour, courtesans appeared on balconies carved in teakwood above the crowded shops and houses below, seeking to attract the attention of pedestrians to their respective dwelling.

Insha Allah Khan, fiery poet and grammarian, must have had one of these women on his mind when he wrote before his death in 1817 about the extreme sensitivity of the wondrous rose that loses colour even as the morning air breezes past it gently:

Nazaaqat uss gul-e-raana ki dekhiyo 'Insha'
Nasim-e-subah jo chhu jaaye rang ho maila

It was the culture of the courtesans to welcome and to spend time with people from all walks of life and to cater to the need of every taste. The well-known courtesans in the old Chowk Bazaar area were a favourite of the wealthy. The less popular and less talented (courtesans) were relegated to serving citizens of a humbler social status, and their brothels were lined up on the outskirts of the imperial city of Lucknow. The courtesans were a (diverse) community of diverse individuals. They came from different ethnic and economic backgrounds. It is possible that social unrest in northern India may have forced women to migrate to Lucknow to earn a living. Although they came from different parts of the region to Lucknow, all differences of language and faith dissolved amongst them and most of them chose to follow the Shia Muslim faith. In the nineteenth century, 85 per cent of the courtesans in Lucknow were Shia Muslims either by birth or through conversion because they wanted to feel closer to each other as members of one community, and also close to the Shia elite that was in power at the time.

For long, people of Persian origin were employed by the Mughals who were ethnically of Turkic, Mongol and Indian origin. Those of Persian origin had suppressed their Shia way of life. Avadh provided its rulers of Persian origin the freedom to revisit the Shia interpretation of Islam. Inspired by his Persian heritage that had roots in the Iranian city of Nishapur, Asaf-ud-Daula asserted his Shia roots with gay abandon and the courtiers were happy to emulate him. It was the desire of Asaf-ud-Daula to mark Lucknow as a Shia Muslim capital in India. The grand imambara built by Asaf-ud-Daula is a powerful symbol of the Shia identity. The imambara or house of the *imam* (the leader) is a Shia institution for believers to congregate and to recall the martyrdom of Imam Husain, the grandson of Muhammad, the Prophet of Islam. By the middle of the nineteenth century, thousands of imambaras had been built in every neighbourhood by Shia Muslims, Sunni Muslims and also by Hindu devotees of Imam Husain. This is how a slice of the Persian way of life nurtured in the lap of the Sassanid, Abbasid and Safavid dynasties trickled into Lucknow where everyone who so desired was welcomed into its fold. If the whole city was busy adopting the Shia way of life, could the courtesans be far behind?

During the mourning period observed by the Shia in the lunar months of Muharram and Chehlum to commemorate the martyrdom of Imam Husain, the courtesans would put away their jewellery and silk and satin clothing, to dress in black. They would go into *azadaari* or mourning and follow the rites and rituals practised during the month of muharram, the new year of the Islamic calendar. The courtesans would no longer dance, but perform *maatam*, the beating of the breast, as they recited poetry in tune to mournful melodies. Instead of singing *malhar*, in celebration of the monsoons, they would recite the *marsiya* or the lamentation at a *majlis* or congregation of mourners, the special religious assemblies held at home and in the imambara. This way, the courtesans continued to earn an income for chanting the soulful *soz* (elegy), *nauha* (the dirge) and the elegy. Thus, the sound of music was never silenced in the city.

Some courtesans who were wealthy enough to do so built their private imambara that was visited by admirers from far and near. The courtesans played a significant role in propagating the Shia faith and in helping to establish Lucknow as the Shia capital of India. By adopting the Shia faith, they had also benefitted from Avadhi Law that allowed *muta* or a temporary marriage between a courtesan and her client.

The reign of Shuja-ud-Daula in Faizabad had encouraged the courtesan to Persianise herself by adopting and practising the Iranian way of life. She was pampered by her admirers at court, which prompted the Persianised courtesan culture to become an accepted way of life. The nobility prided itself on having a beauty from the bazaar as a companion, so knowing a courtesan was considered fashionable. Courtesans were highly respected at court, and some were powerful enough to influence the politics of the day. The courtesan was perhaps the only economically independent woman in the society of that time with a household and income of her own. After the death of Shuja-ud-Daula in 1775, when the capital of Avadh moved from Faizabad, the courtesans too danced their way into Lucknow where the city's desire for endless pleasure was reflected in the poetry and literature of the times.

Insha rejoices over the fate of the rose bud whose lap is favoured by the morning breeze and which is visited by one angel after another:

Ghuncha-e-gul ke saba goad bhari jaati hai
Ek pari aati hai aur ek pari jaati hai

Insha is puzzled. From where, for god's sake, does this fire of love descend? Does it rise from the earth or has it descended from the universe in a whirl?

Zamiin se uthi hai ya charkh par se utri hai
Yeh aag ishq ki ya Rabb kidhar se utri hai

The rulers of Lucknow had made uneasy peace with the British who promised that they would 'always' defend the dynasty and the territory of Avadh. The rulers believed the British when they assured security to the province. They befriended the British and allowed them a permanent residence in Lucknow. It is from the Residency that the British kept a close watch on the disorderly finances of Avadh and used one excuse after another to confiscate local property. However, Lucknow also felt comforted by the presence of the British in considerable strength at a time when Delhi was lawless and many other parts of the country were mired in unrest. Not having to prepare for battles anymore, the elite found lots of time to enjoy a leisurely lifestyle and to enjoy such pleasure that Lucknow became the envy of the world, as a wonderland.

In comparison to Delhi, the Mughal capital, and Calcutta, the British East India Company capital, Lucknow was a pleasure garden perpetually in bloom and a paradise of peace and prosperity.

Writes Asaf-ud-Daula that friends, if you have someone to love, springtime in the home is superior to that of paradise.

Jis jis ke paas doston jis jis ka yaar hai
Behtar chaman se ghar mein issi ke bahaar hai

The Urdu poetry written at the turn of the eighteenth century under the patronage of the Shia Muslim rulers of Lucknow of Persian origin is entertaining, indecent, licentious, sentimental, suggestive and profound in the form of the marsiya.

Asaf-ud-Daula is playful when he says, 'These are all excuses to not come, your home is not that far from where I live':

Yeh na aane ke bahaane hai 'Insha' bhi varna
Miyaan itna toh ghar se mere kuchh nahin ghar dur tera

After the death of Asaf-ud-Daula in 1797, it took more than half a century for poetry in Lucknow to elevate their obsession with the physical attributes of the (seductive) earthly beloved to contemplate on (preoccupy the mind with) the unimaginable beauty of the creator of the world. Along with his admiration for the material world, the poet's spiritual musings gave birth to the devotional genre of marsiya writing. A marsiya is a dirge for Imam Husain, the martyr. The marsiya had flourished in the Deccan. Sauda composed many powerful verses in memory of the martyrs of Karbala even before he came to live in Lucknow. Sauda died in Lucknow in 1780 after having established the tradition of composing the marsiya in six-line stanzas. A marsiya is a six-line unit with a rhyming quatrain and a couplet. It is characterised by six-line verses in an AA, AA and BB rhyme scheme, revolving around the tragic end of Husain, the younger grandson of Muhammad, the Prophet of Islam.

The description here is of that decisive day when Husain left for the battlefield in the desert at noon, with none to help him mount his steed in Karbala, loneliness his sole companion in the midst of the sand dunes. Four-year-old Sakina dusted her father's cape consumed with sadness as Karbala's lion heart stood before her, his head bowed, in silence and alone. Husain's sister stepped forward to help him mount the warhorse with a sigh and a groan.

Husain jab ke chale baad-e dopahar rann ko
Na thha koi ke jo thhaame rakaab-e tausan ko
Sakina jhaad rahi thhi abba ke daaman ko
Husain chup ke khade thhe jhukaaye gardan ko
Na aasra thha koi shah-e-karbalaai ko
Faqat behen ne savaar kiya thha bhai ko

The seed of marsiya writing was sown in Faizabad, and *marsiagoi*, the art of composing elegies, attained maturity in Lucknow in the works of Mir Anees and Mirza Salaamat Ali Dabeer.

The six-line stanza in which the marsiya was written in a style introduced by Sauda is dramatic in form. It is emotional and overflowing with religious content. The great marsiya writers talk of the relationship between the different members of the Prophet's family who were made to suffer in Karbala in such a way that even those listeners with a heart of stone end up shedding copious tears. According to the Shia, shedding tears for Husain open all doors to paradise. There was a time when the poets had the whole city identifying with the suffering of the Prophet's family at the hands of a cruel ruler. This sentiment was the strongest after the British colonised Avadh in 1856 and the last ruler was forced to leave his beloved Lucknow. The marsiya played an important role in arousing patriotism, as the tragedy of the siege of Lucknow by the British was compared to the fate of Imam Husain and his unarmed companions, seventy-two in number, who were attacked by the army of a seventh-century dictator on the battlefield in Karbala. Listening together to the marsiya over and over again united the Muslim and non-Muslim population of the city against British rule in Avadh. This unity is what later merged with the dynamic all-India freedom struggle against colonial rule in the country.

From a short lyrical poem traditionally expressing grief on the martyrdom of Husain, the marsiya was transformed into a lengthy narrative poem by the pen of poet Mir Anees. In the marsiya, Anees writes at length about the battle at Karbala. The poet's patron was the opulent Shia Muslim ruler of Avadh whose ancestors came from Iran, a predominantly Shia country.

Anees was born in Faizabad and died in Lucknow in 1874. He is one of the greatest marsiya writers and had an attractive stage presence and talent for dramatic recitation. The recitations of Anees were heard by spellbound audiences. Every inch of the area around the pulpit where the poet sat was packed to capacity as the poet used words in such a clever way that the audience was transported to the desert town of Karbala beside the River Euphrates where water was denied to the thirsting members of the Prophet's family, including unarmed women and children.

Perched on the topmost step of the pulpit, speaking on behalf of Husain, the poet says that awake at the emergence of the first ray of the sun, scorching even at that hour so early, on this day his life will be sacrificed so that the values of Islam continue to live.

Addressing his family members as brave warriors who have woken up to a day of strife and slaughter when the blood of the family of Muhammad will flow, Husain, the beloved son of Zehra, rises from sleep. His face is flushed like a red rose, and without pain. The night of separation has given way to the day of union. For the family of the Prophet angels mourn, they have spent the night awake and in anguish, in wait for this morn.

Haan ghaaziyon yeh din hai jidaal-e-qataal ka
Yahaan khoon bahega Muhammad ki aal ka
Chehra khushi se surkh hai Zehra ke laal ka
Guzri shab-e-firaaq din aaya visal ka
Hum woh hain gham karenge malak jinke vaaste
Raatein tadapke kaati hain iss din ke vaaste

Returning to the other Mir who had witnessed the ruin of Delhi, and his helplessness, because he could do nothing about it, had made Mir shed tears without stopping. Even after the carnage was over, he continued to cry. He was unable to recognise a single home in the lane where he had once lived. Mir could not trace his former neighbours. Complete strangers told him that they had no clue where he should look for his friends. He walked past one ruined house after another and saw that walls had collapsed, crowded wine shops and the favourite haunt of comely young men and elders had been wiped out, leaving not only Mir's *dilli* (Delhi) but also his *dil* (heart) wounded.

Before coming to Lucknow, Mir had dragged his feet to where he had once lived in Delhi. Here he had laughed together with friends and in the evening recited poetry. Here he had spent time as a lover and was desired by many a beautiful woman for whom he wrote verses. His home was razed to the ground. He stood on a deserted road, silently gazing at nothingness and allowing sorrow to drown his heart. That day he made a promise that as long as he lived, he would never visit Delhi again. On his way out, Mir saw a bird on a bough in the ruined city. He paused to ask the bird, 'What do you have to say about this wilderness?' The bird summed up the sorry state of affairs in Delhi in two words. 'Alas! Alas!'

Mir perhaps learnt how to sigh from this bird. He spent his entire life lamenting his fate and has sprinkled his poetry with a breathless portion of *aah*, making many look upon Mir as a poet most depressive.

Mir had good reasons to nurse his low spirit. He had faced love and loss early in life. He was eleven years old when Mir Abdullah, his father, had passed away. Throughout his life he missed the love, care and knowledge that his father had showered upon him. Mir Abdullah was a religious teacher, and before leaving the world he had taught Mir to value compassion and to realise the worth of love. Except for this lesson in love and longing, there was nothing else that his father had left for Mir. After his father passed away, Mir did not feel at home in Agra. His stepbrother resented him and had made life difficult for Mir in their Agra home. In the blink of an eye, Mir had lost his father, his home and the love of his life who loved him once but was now married.

Taking with him nothing except memories of the time he had spent with his father in Agra, Mir travelled to Delhi to make a living. The boy was wide-eyed as he wandered around the grand capital of Mughal emperors. He described the streets of Delhi like drawings in an album. Whichever page, he said, was turned, there was a painting. As far as Mir was concerned, there could be no place equal to Delhi anywhere in the world. But after Delhi was looted by Persian and Afghan warriors, jackals could be heard howling in the city. For days on end, lamps were not lit in mosques at night. There was light in only one house out of a hundred houses. Fellow poet Mirza Muhammad Rafi Sauda wrote that after Abdali the Afghan was through with ruining Delhi, vermin had crawled in places where people had once enjoyed music, and had welcomed the advent of spring with laughter. Sauda too migrated to Lucknow and died in the city in 1781, leaving behind a solid legacy of literature.

The lovely buildings in Delhi which once made the famished man forget his hunger are in ruins. In the beautiful gardens where nightingales sang love songs to the rose, grass grows waist-high around fallen pillars and ruined arches.

Sauda had wailed that Shahjahanabad did not deserve this terrible fate!

> You [Delhi] who were once vibrant with life, love and hope like the heart of a young lover, you for whom men afloat upon the ocean of the world once set their course as to the promised shore, you from whose dust men came to gather pearls. Not even a lamp of clay now burns where once the chandelier blazed with light all night.

Now Mir mourned his migration to Lucknow. Throughout the journey of more than 500 kilometres, Mir was silent and lost in thought. Mir would sigh from time to time, reminding fellow passengers that he was still in their midst in the ox-drawn carriage. They nudged each other, watching him scribble without stop. Along with a big and dome-shaped turban that reached his brows, Mir wore a frown. He had folded a length of cloth and tied it around his waist, like a belt, and in one hand he held a spear. His other hand poured down words on slips of paper like the flow of never-ending tears. Then he tucked all the paper that he wrote upon under this belt. All this while he was oblivious to the attention he attracted.

Mir was preoccupied with thoughts that meandered between valleys of sorrow and mountains of joy. A particular image returned to elate him, but also to make him weep. Images of a fairy stepping down from the full moon and into his arms looped in his head without pause. But before he could reach out and caress her, the image of the fairy would always disappear. Mir clutched the left side of the chest. He kept trying to snuff out the smoke that he felt rise from the bottom of his heart. He wondered if only his heart was on fire, or was it his whole body?

The fairy continued to haunt Mir as her image flitted in and out of memories of desolate streets he had left behind in

Delhi. It was difficult for him to forget the indignity that a majority of his fellow citizens had been subjected to. He was grateful that he was able to channel the pain and resentment he had experienced throughout his life into poetry, aware that the realm of poetry is not the same as the world of human beings. Poetry thrives on unfulfilled yearnings for a glimpse of the petal-like mouth of the beloved, but in real life human beings pine for a touch and a feel of the body of those they love.

In *The Sun That Rose from the Earth*, the book with the magnificent collection of five stories about Urdu poets by Shamsur Rahman Faruqi, the Urdu critic imagines Mir as a young star rising bright on the horizon at the dawn of Urdu poetry. Mir is madly in love with a beauty from Iran and says in the chapter titled 'In Such Meetings and Partings, Ultimately':

> I want the heart of Nurus Saadat, but only for the duration that she makes her body my body. I should take off her clothes; keep awake the whole night, looking at her bare body. Stupid, am I not?

Faruqi is the author of a four-volume study of Mir. He regrets that critics concentrate only on the sorrowful side of Mir's personality. This stereotypes the poet as someone who did not know how to smile, and if he did smile it seemed as if it was by mistake. After Faruqi read Mir again and again, he discovered a person and poet most spirited. Faruqi compares Mir's vivacity to that of Shakespeare, a formidably complex character who is capable of giving words to any feeling, any thought, any sensation, any mood, with equal facility and felicity, including all the crude thoughts that cross the mind.

Mir was a prolific writer, but at some stage in the history of Urdu, it became a habit with critics to quote only sad verses penned by the poet. Mir's vast body of work includes a rainbow of emotions. His verses are achingly romantic, erotic, teasing and even vulgar. All of Mir has to be read to know what a colourful personality he was.

Mir explores the idea of God and spirituality with as much ease as matters of human misery and injustice on earth. When Mir expresses deep concern for the condition of human existence, he does sound depressing like when he says, behind the veil of poetry, I have expressed my sorrow a lot and the elegy has made my heart weep as well, a lot:

Sher ke parde mein maine gham sunaaya hai bahot
Marsiya ne dil ko mere bhi rulaaya hai bahot

Mir did bring his melancholia with him to Lucknow, but the lush landscape and the local language of Avadhi charmed him when he had first visited Lucknow in 1748, although not enough to have made him want to stay on in the city. He was twenty-five years old at that time and the vocabulary he heard local people speak in Avadh had gradually snuck into his poetry to purge his writing of constant references to the unfamiliar landscape and metaphors borrowed from faraway Iran, and from the land of the Arab people.

In the accent of an Avadhi, Mir writes that if he had only known, he would not have fallen in love with anyone but taken that desire of his heart with him to the grave:

Hum jaante toh ishq na karte kisi ke saath
Le jaate dil ko khaak mein iss aarzu ke saath

He had felt at home in the local dialect that people spoke in Agra, Delhi and Lucknow. Mir's ideas and thoughts remained complex. His poetic expression of the mysteries of life was penned down in simple everyday language and that made people read his poetry over and over again. Mir's thoughts and the way he uses language continues to inspire all lovers of poetry, although in some it evokes more of a sigh of *aah* in comparison to many more *waah* reserved for other poets.

It is possible to elicit many more waahs for Mir's poetry, but only after going through it all. Mir is an exhilarating poet who is able to thrill his audience like none other. Mir is also an amazing person who confesses that he often feels drawn to the worst in society. That feeling about himself makes him doubt his values and he wonders what he stands for in life. He finds it difficult to believe that he is the same person who is aware of a treasure trove of beautiful vocabulary which he is able to weave into magnificent verses, and the one who also writes that if I cannot have you, your brother will do, for when I love it does not matter who the beloved is:

Vey nahin toh unka bhai aur
Ishq karne ki kya manaai hai

Reading everything that Mir has written will reveal his sense of humour, his anger, his bawdy verses full of bad words, his lust, his self-love and his tremendous ability to laugh at himself. Mir is sensual as well, and it is rewarding to take the trouble of discovering Mir in his entirety and on one's own. Most people take the shortcut of reading Mir as suggested in bits and pieces by others. To find out different aspects of Mir is an exercise most exciting. It is sheer joy to chance upon a playful mood of Mir, like when he is amazed at his extreme innocence for accepting medicine from the same son of the perfumer who is responsible for having made the poet ill in the first place.

'Mir' kya saade hain beemar hue jiske sabab
Ussi attar ke laundey se dawaa lete hain

Mir's lesser-known verses include the poet's extreme honesty. Mir is frank about his desperate desire to hold the beloved in his arms and to make love to her naked body. Mir is also good at quarrelling with the beloved and not always does he praise her beauty. He often calls her names when annoyed. But once convinced, he is also humble enough to acknowledge the individual worth of the woman he loves.

In *The Sun That Rose from the Earth*, Faruqi concludes:

> 'Mir' was not the same Mir now, but what he'd lost were his angularities. Nurus Saadat's love taught him humility, at least in the presence of love. He joked and played the games still, especially chess, of which he was something of a master. But he also knew that he was small. He could write any kind of poetry, but he could not command his kind of woman.

Mir Taqi Mir

Dekh toh dil ki jaan se uthta hai
Yeh dhuan sa kahaan se uthta hai
Gor kis diljale ki hai yeh falak

Shola ik subah yaan se uthta hai
Khaana-e-dil se zeenahar na ja
Koi aise makaan se uthta hai
Naala sar kheenchta hai jab mera
Shor ek aasmaan se uthta hai
Ladti hai uski chashm-e-shok jahaan
Ek aashob vaan se uthta hai
Sudh le ghar ki bhi shola-e-awaaz
Duud kuchh aashiyaan se uthta hai
Baithne kaun de hai phir usko
Jo tir e aastaan se uthta hai
Yun uthe aah uss gali se hum
Jaise koi jahaan se uthta hai
Ishq ek 'mir' bhaari patthar hai
Kab yeh tujh naa-tavaan se uthta hai

Watch it rise from the hearth of the heart. From where else does this smoke arise?
What soul is buried here that flames the sky every morning with rising envy?
Beloved, leave not the heart, does anyone abandon a home like this?
When the head held up high implores, restlessness rises in heaven.
When the wandering look of the beloved clashes with another, tears arise.
Your fury and your fire will burn down the dwelling, there is smoke rising from the home.
Who else will entertain the one turned away from your doorstep,

when I leave the lane of the lover a sigh springs up
like a farewell to life.
Who returns once risen from your doorstep when
I leave the lane of the lover, a sigh rises like a
farewell to life.
Love, 'Mir', is heavy as a stone; it is not for a
weakling like you.

TWO

Mushaira

Sirajuddin Ali Khan Arzu, seniormost poet in Persian, had mentored many Urdu poets, including Mir. Arzu was an uncle of Mir and he had amended the younger poet's verses in Delhi. Arzu died in 1756, decades before Mir came to live in Lucknow in 1782. Arzu's mortal remains were taken from Lucknow as he had wished to be buried in Delhi.

The home of Arzu's ancestors was Agra, but he had loved his life in Delhi and nursed a special affection for it. However, circumstances did not allow him to live in Delhi after a while. When he could no longer earn a living in Delhi, Arzu decided to move elsewhere. Arzu was a linguist and lexicographer. Shuja-ud-Daula, the ruler of Avadh, was an ardent admirer of his scholarship. Shuja-ud-Daula was the father of Asaf-ud-Daula and his capital city was Faizabad. Considering his knowledge of Persian, Arabic and Sanskrit, Shuja-ud-Daula offered Arzu employment at his court where Arzu encouraged budding poets to write in Urdu.

That lesson of Arzu had sparked an intense burst of

interest in a new poetic genre that was Persian in style but linguistically indigenous. In those days, the new language was called rekhta or mixture, as it was a collection of vocabulary from many different languages. Over time, the founders of rekhta did such a splendid job of putting together a brand-new language that eventually Urdu became a craze. The name Urdu was used for rekhta only towards the end of the nineteenth century.

As Arzu got older, he increasingly felt that it was time to move away from the Persian language. Persian was a sweet song of nightingales from the garden of Iran, and however beautiful, it was the property of others. There is an incident that Arzu did not forget. Once a visitor from Persia had mocked the Persian written in India. He found Arzu's knowledge of Persian reeking of *kachauri*, a heavily spiced, deep-fried savoury found in the Indian kitchen. The arrogance of the Persian had hurt Arzu and it made him think about writing in Urdu. His dream was to bring such radiance to the new Indian language so that it could compare with Persian, and eventually make Persian fall into disuse in India.

Sauda had moved to Lucknow in 1772, nearly two decades after the death of Arzu, his mentor. He was the court poet of Asaf-ud-Daula who provided for him generously. Sauda originally wrote in Persian, but on the insistence of Arzu he began to write in the new language. Sauda was one of the most important founding elders to compose in rekhta. Here is a tongue-in-cheek complaint by Sauda to the beloved. She is addressed as the wealthy owner of a garden, showering flowers and also fruits upon others as the poet says—then why not favour him too?

Gul phenke hain auron ki taraf balki samar bhi
Ae khaana-bar-andaaz-e-chaman kuchh toh idhar bhi

Sauda is the first to perfect the qasida in the present form of writing an ode. He wrote ghazals too, but is most admired for his stinging satires. Sauda is the first to take the art of satire seriously and his writing is full of fire and wit that provides much merriment and laughter, also contradicting the perception that Urdu poetry is only about the cry of the heart and about complaints in life.

Sauda is remembered as the happy-go-lucky son of an affluent father who became famous rather quickly. His father was a *saudagar* or merchant and it is from there that the poet chose the pen name of Sauda.

He used local vocabulary to say that one might be attentive to his words or not, but what concerns Sauda is to have his say.

Tum kaan dhar suno na suno usske harf ko
'Sauda' ko haigi apni hi guftaar se gharaz

The satires of Sauda were so biting that everyone avoided being on the wrong side of the poet. When Sauda was annoyed, he would insult the enemy with words. His pen spared no one, whether learned, ignorant, poor, rich, good or bad. When he started berating someone his words chased the person so relentlessly that he grew tired of life. Sauda had a servant called Ghuncha who was the keeper of the poet's pen-case. When Sauda was angry with someone he would call Ghuncha and ask for his pen and begin to write against the one who had annoyed him at the speed of Satan.

Now poetry was no longer only about mysticism and religion. From the eighteenth-century, poets were exploring many other down-to-earth themes as well, apart from spirituality. Today, Sauda's reputation rests not on love lyrics or ghazals, but on the brilliant wordplay of his satires.

Arzu wrote in Persian, but towards the end of his life he played with Urdu vocabulary. He says that ever since he dared to visit the one so passionate, the whole world is witness to his courage:

Uss tund-khu sanam se milne laga hoon jab se
Har koi jaanta hai meri dilaavari ko

Writes Muhammad Husain Azad in his seminal book *Aab-e-Hayat* (The Water of Life):

> Arzu can make the same claim on the Urdu language that Aristotle can make on the philosophy of logic. As long as all logisticians will be called the descendants of Aristotle, all Urdu speakers will be called the descendants of Khan-e-Arzu ...

Published in 1880, *The Water of Life* is an important first book on the history of Urdu. The author continues to praise Arzu, saying that his training had nurtured sophisticated offsprings who were able to cook up a literary concoction. The language was local, but the style and manner of expression was Persian. More than a century after the death of Arzu, Azad wrote that his mad heart remembers the many good things that he had heard his elders say about Arzu. He had kept all the information about Arzu in his heart till he was able to write it down in *The Water of Life*.

At the heart of the ancient *ustad–shagird* or master–pupil tradition of north India was the process of correction by the ustad who tried to improve the shagird's poetry. The most common kind of rectification involved changing only a word or two, and the main goal of the changes was generally to make the two lines of the verse more tightly connected. Mir and Sauda were both corrected by Arzu. The other tradition cultivated and cherished by Urdu poets were poetic recitations and discussions at a mushaira. Mir remembered all the mushaira sessions hosted by Arzu, and he held similar mushaira gatherings at his own residence following the same etiquette.

For Mir, the mushaira was a unique north Indian tradition. The first mushaira was hosted by Mir in Delhi on the recommendation of Dard. Mir had venerated Dard and was happy to follow in his footsteps. After the mushaira at Mir's place, Dard had renounced the world and preoccupied himself with mysticism. Thus, the tradition of hosting a mushaira on the fifteenth day of every month ended. Dard had asked Mir to change the venue of the mushaira to his home. Mir mentions many more mushaira sessions held in different homes in Delhi.

> Four or five years ago, there used to be a gathering of rekhta companions at Jafar Ali Khan's house. God knows what happened that caused it to break up. In the old days, for several months, the poet Kafir had fixed a gathering for rekhta at his house; finally, his rakish habits caused it to break up. I used to see the poet Ajiz in Hafiz Halim's mushaira.

By the early nineteenth century, Avadh was politically independent of Delhi, and its prosperity allowed the city to provide generous patronage to poets, writers and scholars of Urdu and Persian. The migration of poets and scholars eastward from Delhi only helped Lucknow to emerge as the new centre of Urdu literary life. Like its governor, the language too was free of allegiance to Delhi. The first flowering of Urdu poetry had already occurred in the kingdoms of Bijapur and Golconda, followed by a second development at Aurangabad. The third and the most glorious phase for Urdu was in Delhi, before the scene moved to Lucknow. The language was in use much before it was favoured by the court, during the unavoidable interaction between the speakers of Persian and Turkic dialects, and the speakers of various Indian vernaculars. For centuries, a Persian milieu had ruled over north India when Persian was the official language of court, justice and bureaucracy, as well as of poetry.

Initially, the mushaira was nothing but a meeting of a close circle of poets who recited verses in Persian, the mother tongue of many Indian Muslims of Turkic, Afghan and Iranian origin. Over time Arzu's wish was fulfilled, and Persian lost its position to rekhta.

The flowering of the rekhta poetic tradition in north India had coincided with the Delhi visit of the celebrated Vali Aurangabadi in the early eighteenth century. Vali came to north India with his collection of the ghazal written in the vernacular. It is safe to presume that many a mushaira was hosted for Vali in Delhi to recite his love lyrics. Vali recited that those who seek paradise in this life should take a look at the charisma of her face:

Chahta hai iss jahaan mein gar bahisht
Ja tamasha dekh uss rukhsaar ka

Till then, the new language was viewed as common speech. But following Vali's example, and bowled over by the beauty of his lyrics, poets in Delhi began to write not only in Persian, but also in rekhta. Soon the face of the earth in this part of the world crawled with rekhta poets who met regularly at a mushaira and who are responsible for elevating the poetic status of rekhta to that of Persian. The mushaira had mainly featured Urdu poetry, although conversations continued to be laced in Persian phrases as knowledge of Persian was still considered a proof of being educated. In Lucknow, the mushaira enjoyed mass popularity. It was a favoured form of cultural recreation throughout the city and every neighbourhood held its own mushaira, infusing a love of Urdu poetry amongst the rich and poor of the city.

Here is a description of a mushaira by Urdu critic Muhammad Husain Azad:

> Look—the gathering of the mushaira is adorned with nobles and aristocrats. Sober elders and young men sit side by side dressed in long robes and heavy turbans. Someone has only a dagger, someone else has strapped on a sword. Some are so elderly that white beards have made their old age radiant. Some, in their youthfulness, have happened to bid farewell to their beards—now how should they wear beards, for the law of consistency of style would be broken...

Every mushaira ended with the same cry in each heart to the sun, to not rise till eternity. The yearning was that the night never end, and the gathering of innumerable poets without count never disperse. The poets at the mushaira seemed to be as many as the stars in the sky. The enthusiasm of the listeners was always flowing over and candle after candle would fizzle out but never the flame of passion for poetry.

The poets recited what they had composed but many a voice would also recite from the work of Delhi poets like Khwaja Mir Dard, displaying a reluctance on the part of the emigrants to cut the umbilical cord with Delhi. The *saqi* was requested to begin the bustle of departure, but the bearer of wine kept the wine flask circulating for as long as it was possible to do so. The host tried to understand which way the people's hearts led because there was always the fear that people might get impatient, become restless and slip out of hand. Then what? A seasoned *nazim* knew when to say, 'Enough, the mushaira has ended', and the rest of the art was left for another night. Pointing to the colour of the dawn, resisting a long speech and requesting all whether intoxicated with speech or asleep, to arise. Arise. It is over and the sun has come down upon the head.

The origins of the word mushaira are traced to *shaara* in Arabic, meaning to feel, to know, to learn and to compose verses. And to know in such a way as to be enchanted, and to be able to cast a spell with a verse. No wonder the entire city was drowned in an unbridled craze for mushaira. Citizens had lived to go from one mushaira to another, dreaming, discussing and reciting lyrics. The mushaira had provided complete entertainment, both intellectual and emotional, and the gathering of poetry lovers was also an invite to the anonymous for spontaneous recitations. The mushaira was held at the house of a poet or his friend, at a palace of a patron, a nobleman, or at a haveli, a luxurious spacious mansion of an aristocrat. The host was almost always a respected citizen, not necessarily a poet himself but one who loved poetry, a literary critic and with a reputation amongst well-known poets. Just in case the host was young and inexperienced, those who had more knowledge guided him in the way a mushaira is organised.

The planning for a mushaira was meticulous from the start. Much time and energy were spent on queries like where would it be held, and who would make it to the guest list. It was important to choose the correct *nazim*, the person who would preside over the mushaira. The *nazim* had to be witty and sensitive to the feelings of the poets and the audience at a mushaira.

In Lucknow, every evening brought an invitation to a new mushaira in a different part of the city. Streets leading to the venue of the mushaira were decked up like a bride. The venue was lined up with hundreds of lanterns and lamps were lit below colourful tents inside the *shamiana*. The floors were covered in carpets, cushions and pillows in wait for ustads to take their place with their many shagirds sitting around them. In wait for the poet was also a gigantic candle, that essential shama, standing below a lampshade called a *fanus*. According to tradition, the host received every guest and seated him accordingly. The poets sat in a circle or facing each other while the listeners sat behind the poets. Before taking their place, the poets engaged in ceremonial greetings, bowing and informally murmuring conversation with each other. Both the poets and guests were always dressed in their

Sunday best. It was also the tradition to greet each other by standing upright with the right hand raised to the ear, as if about to begin a prayer.

At the start of the mushaira, the nizam signalled for the candle stand to be placed before a poet who would either recite, or inaugurate the evening in *tarannum*, a style of singing. The recitation was repeatedly interrupted with different words of praise by the audience. The air echoed with loud sounds of *subhanallah*, *mukarrar* and *irshad* from different corners where a mushaira was held, invariably at a palace with a huge assembly hall, or a big house with a spacious courtyard and attended by Muslims and non-Muslims alike. A mushaira began with the presentation of compositions by younger poets, most of them disciples to renowned ustads. To strengthen the confidence of the young poets, everyone cried bravo even when the recitation was mediocre. When known poets took to the floor, it was always amidst great enthusiasm expressed in abundance by the audience. Finally, when the candle and the lamps were about to die out, the most loved and revered ustad would appear to end the mushaira with his recitations. The king at the mushaira was always the one who had received the most praise and requests to repeat his verses. Many would copy copiously the recitations of their favourite poet in little notebooks called *bayaz*. An important feature of the mushaira remains its democratic character that continues to welcome all poetry lovers irrespective of caste, creed, or gender to this day.

The mushaira had enjoyed mass popularity in Lucknow as a favourite form of cultural recreation among all strata of educated urban dwellers. A mushaira was held everywhere and catered to different poetic tastes, and requirements of the literati and connoisseurs. To this day the mushaira is solely responsible for nourishing and keeping the Urdu language alive. It is at a mushaira where poetry lovers of the future are allowed to flower.

Burhan-ul-mulk Saadat Ali Khan, founder of the Avadh dynasty, who had conquered Lucknow but chose to focus his activities in Faizabad near Ayodhya, was a great host. Urdu poetry had inspired his policy of the essential unity of all life, however diverse and oppositional it looked at first sight. This attitude towards life stems from the mystical belief in *wahdat al wajud* or oneness of being practised by both the *sant* (saint) and the *sufi* (mystic) in Avadh. Saadat Ali Khan brought some of these ideas with him from Iran and from his ancestors of the Safavid dynasty. A Kurdish mystic had founded the Safavid dynasty in the fourteenth century. A century later, Iran was converted to a Shia Muslim kingdom by the Safavid rulers who believed in Shia concepts like the imam, a community leader.

Saadat Ali Khan taught his descendants to befriend dissidents as the absence of conflict helped rulers to consolidate power over territory that they conquer. That is how literary life and liberal ideas in the newly independent province of Avadh were able to thrive in an atmosphere of comfort and comparative peace. After his death, the presence of Safdarjung, son-in-law of Saadat Ali Khan, added more Shia flavour to Muslim neighbourhoods, and Safdarjung's son Shuja-ud-Daula built Faizabad into a grand seat of Shia power. Faizabad became home of Sirajuddin Khan Arzu, Mirza Muhammad Rafi Sauda and Syed Muhammad Mir Soz, all of whom worked to develop

Urdu into a literary language of great distinction.

Poet Mir Hasan, famous for his *masnavi*, the long narrative poems, visited Faizabad with his father during the lifetime of Safdarjung and Shuja-ud-Daula. Mir Hasan wrote that Faizabad was full of wide-open streets like lines on a white piece of paper. The bazaars had overflowed with jewels, cloth merchants, money changers and metalworkers. The commercial prosperity of Faizabad was impressive, and there were flower and fruit shops and sweetmeats like phirni and faluda. There were kebabs of different varieties and many places to socialise, like coffee shops and corners, where prostitutes and young boys from Kashmir had entertained. The dresses and ornaments worn especially by the women of Faizabad had dazzled Mir Hasan. He found the women flirtatious and perfumed in *itr* of sandal essence, and their clothing had revealed their breasts with great generosity.

Compared to Lucknow, the poet who had moved from Delhi found Faizabad a commercial, culinary and erotic paradise. The heat, dust and armies of ants had disgusted the poet in Lucknow. The Shia Mir Hasan even compared Lucknow to Kufa, in modern-day Iraq, near the desert town of Karbala where Imam Husain, grandson of Muhammad, the Prophet of Islam, was beheaded in the seventh century by a cruel dictator. Mir Hasan complains of the miserliness of the people in Lucknow, its vulnerability to attacks by wild animals like wolves and the yearly flooding of River Gomti.

With one's nostrils full of mud, what poetry can one write? Mir Hasan cried. (From the English translation of *Ab-e-Hayat* by Muhammad Husain Azad).

After his move to Lucknow, Mir Hasan had missed Faizabad

and pleaded with the saqi to quickly fill his goblet and row his boat to the other side. The narrow lanes of Lucknow had suffocated the poet, and each hillock sat like a rock on his chest. Waves from the Gomti came up to beat at his breast, he claimed, to say why not travel to Faizabad. And that is what the poet did. He went back to Faizabad and as soon as he had entered that town, it felt as if heaven's door had opened for him.

Here Mir Hasan complains of Lucknow before Asaf-ud-Daula had moved from Faizabad to make it his capital in 1775 (This is an incident from the English translation of *Ab-e-Hayat* by Muhammad Husain Azad). It is said that whatever Shuja-ud-Daula had achieved in Faizabad paled into insignificance in comparison to the way his son Asaf-ud-Daula developed Lucknow. Later, Mir Hasan even softens the tone of his criticism. He notes that a few generous patrons have settled in the town, even if most of them have their origins in Delhi. One of them was Khwaja Basit, a man of great generosity.

He concedes that Asaf-ud-Daula had improved the city by way of constructing great public buildings and imposing some order on a somewhat chaotic place like Lucknow. Asaf-ud-Daula's buildings had the whole world in raptures. Asaf-ud-Daula had put an end to all the dirt and beautified Lucknow like a garden.

Many of Lucknow's palaces, mosques and imambaras, the Shia religious congregational halls are from the era of Asaf-ud-Daula whose court had welcomed people of talent from all over the world. To this day, the eighteenth-century ruler is remembered in the city for his generosity and liberality, making people say that if God forgets, it is Asaf-ud-Daula who provides for the people.

Jisko na de maula
Usko de Asaf-ud-Daula

Like so many other talented people, Ghulam Rasul and Miyaan Jani had moved from Faizabad to Lucknow. The two had specialised in qawwali performances, the devotional genre of vocal music introduced in Delhi in the fourteenth century by Amir Khusrau, the poet, scholar, singer, musician and spiritual devotee of Nizamuddin Aulia. In Lucknow, Ghulam Rasul and Miyaan Jani performed the qawwali but were also inspired to interpret the more meditative genre of vocal music called khayal. Rasul's son Miyaan Shori continued to innovate, and was in demand for singing the tappa, a light classical form of music.

So electrifying was the cultural milieu of nineteenth-century Lucknow that it began to the Delhi that once was—a Delhi far more uninhibited, far more culturally confident, far more sophisticated, far more intellectually vibrant than it ever was: when women could flirt and make love with men or other women, and so could the men; when a life of sensations went hand in hand with a life of thoughts, with no sense of incongruity.

Asaf-ud-Daula

Zindagi
Humne qissa bahut kaha dil ka
Na suna tumne maajra dil ka

Apne matlab ki sab hi kehte hain
Hai nahin koi aashna dil ka
Ishq mein aisi khinchi rusvaai
Ho gaya shor ja baja dil ka
Iss qadar behavaas rehta hai
Jaise kuchh koi le gaya dil ka
Ek bose pe bechte thhe hum
Tu-ne sauda na kuchh kiya dil ka
Tere milne se faayda kya hai
Na ho haasil jo mudda dil ka
Kyun diya 'Asif' uss sitamgar ko
Aap tu muddai hua dil ka

Life,
I have always talked about the story of my heart
You did not listen to the heart
Everyone says what is of interest to them
None is familiar with the heart
In love I was so disgraced
Openly abused was the heart
It suffered pangs
As if it had lost something of the heart
A kiss was enough to sell it to you
But you did not bargain with the heart
What is the use of meeting you
When affairs remain unsettled of the heart
Why did you, 'Asif', give to the cruel one?
Now it is you who is enemy of the heart.

THREE

Mushafi

Mir Taqi Mir was the sun and moon of every mushaira in Lucknow which was his home for nearly three decades before his death in 1810. Mir was celebrated for beading words into poems, as if a necklace of pearls. Mir's admirers were like bees to honey. Mir's poetry stole the heart of many more people, including those who were not well-versed in Persian. If previous centuries had fed the flowering of Persian verses, now was the time to salute sensitivities in one's own mother tongue known in different parts of north India as khadi boli, hindavi, rekhta and, later, as Urdu.

The nineteenth century had already dawned to slow down the walk of the octogenarian wonder, but not Mir's passion for poetry. Mir arrived at yet another mushaira where the lanterns were up in the courtyard, the carpets and pillows were spread below, and the scent of sandalwood was everywhere. A crowd of people appeared to pay their respect, and to seat Mir in the centre of the mushaira.

There was innumerable talent in attendance. Unusual

people, lively and full of vitality, hovered around Mir. There was laughter as poet after poet took their place at the site of the most-awaited event that took place every evening after dinner. This was followed by poetry recitations and musical performances by dancing girls who kept the city awake till after dawn.

Nobles and aristocrats had trooped in. The gathering was a mix of individuals. There were elderly poets dressed in long robes and wearing heavy turbans, their snow-white beards adding a glow to their ageing cheeks, while some of the younger did not sport a beard. But what was common was that everyone sat side by side. Some had a dagger strapped to the waist, others a sword. Female lovers of poetry and poets participated in the electric evening from a place hidden from view. From where they sat, the women could see the spectacle, but none from the floor of the mushaira could see them.

A moment arrived when conversation held its breath and heads turned towards a newcomer with coal black eyes. Recently landed from Delhi, Shaikh Hamdani Mushafi looked for a place to sit. His presence further fanned the warm ambience of the mushaira that already resembled a genial embrace. Mushafi caressed his silken beard, unaware that a few ringlets of his long black hair had escaped out of the paper-thin and *chikan*-embroidered cap on his head. The rest of his hair was combed in a long braid. The women watching him through the crack in their secret chamber swooned. They predicted that it would not take too long for this charismatic personality to charm the city. The women had heard that Mushafi was fond of wrestling, and that he was a regular at a local *akhara*. That is why his wrists were wide and powerful.

They tried to imagine the strength of his full arms, straight shoulders and high neck.

A group of usherers escorted Mushafi to a spot on the carpet where people sat supported by bolsters in snow-white cotton covers placed against the wall. Mushafi made himself comfortable. He held the mouthpiece of a hookah in his left hand as he accepted the cone of a betel leaf wrapped in a sheet of silver with the right hand.

The candle was placed before a youngster who was showered with applause for his recitation. Then followed poet after poet, each one of them dripping verses like dew upon the evening.

When it was his turn, Mushafi read, and Mir was attentive. Mushafi continued with more recitations. It is well known that the accomplishments of others were often invisible to Mir. Mir was not known to be generous with praise for the work of others. It almost seemed that Mir considered it a sin to nod in appreciation of other poets. Once a teenager from a family of noblemen from Panipat district had requested Mir to correct his writing. Mir's response was, 'Sayed Sahab, Urdu is the language of Delhi alone. Please don't bother yourself about it. Please just keep composing in your own Persian-Wersian.'

Shaikh Imam Baksh Nasikh was nearly half a century younger to Mir. Once he had mustered up enough courage and taken his verses for Mir to read. Nasikh was surprised and hurt when Mir refused to even look at his poetry. He came away deeply disappointed. He consoled himself by saying that Mir Sahab is a great poet, but no angel. He is only human. Nasikh decided to re-read his verses and to correct his work himself.

To Saadat Yaar Khan Rangin, one of the greatest poets of nineteenth-century Lucknow, Mir had said once, 'Young sir, you are the son of a nobleman. Please take up spear-throwing and archery. Please practise horsemanship. Poetry is the act of lacerating the heart and burning the liver. Please don't even come near it. Your temperament is not suited to this art. It is not something that you will learn. What is the point of wasting your and my time to no purpose?'

Once Mir was asked to name those he considered poets. He named Sauda and himself. After a pause he added the name of Khwaja Mir Dard, who he felt was only half a poet.

'And Mir Soz, the mentor of Asaf-ud-Daula ruler of Lucknow?' was the next question. Mir heard the question and frowned. He said, 'Is Mir Soz Sahab a poet? Well, taking that into account, there are exactly two and three-quarter poets in the city.'

That is why Mushafi was over the moon when Mir interrupted his recitation and asked him to repeat the last couplet at this mushaira. Mushafi promptly did. That request to him from Mir was worth a thousand praises from others. Mushafi accepted the response from Mir as confirmation of his poetic talent. He stood up and saluted Mir repeatedly saying that in his musings he would remember to mention beside this verse how Mir had made him recite it twice.

Shaikh Ghulam Hamdani chose as his pen name 'Mushafi' meaning one who is of the Holy Book. Although no one ever saw Mushafi read any holy book, or observe religious rituals like praying regularly or fasting, he would often say that it is the human being that is worthy of marvel. Respect for life was his worship. In his seventh collection of works he wrote that differences of faith and religion robbed spirituality of its purity. There are a hundred pitchers for sure, but the water drawn into the different pitchers is from the same river on the same bank.

Mushafi read all kinds of books and was interested in philosophy. He concluded that rationality is a gift to humans. He made his loved ones apologise to God on his behalf when they heard him say that the ultimate mischief of creation was to have been pronounced "to be" one day. With a twinkle in the eyes, Mushafi said that the universe came to be without saying 'why'. Watching the cruelty and hate practised around him, Mushafi sometimes wondered if the world was not managed by demons, instead of gods.

Mushafi had puzzled everyone when one day he praised the clergy, and the next day he was critical of the same Shia leadership called imam. His attitude towards Sunni Muslims was the same. Sometimes he wrote elegies in favour of mystics, and sometimes he was critical of the existing sycophancy and hypocrisy even amongst the Sufi mystics.

It was not the different religious beliefs that bothered him, but the nonchalant practice of brutality by human beings. The many wrongs in society and a lack of social justice made Mushafi angry. Mushafi is accused of selling his poetry to make ends meet and of allowing others to put their name to his poetry in return for money. This may or may not be true, but chroniclers of his time mention Mushafi as a generous person who was deeply affectionate towards his students, and kind towards those in distress. He never denied help to anyone in need, believing that love for human beings was the true love of God. Mushafi believed that God lives in the human heart and not in some non-human space built by man with brick and mortar.

Mushafi said that he would sacrifice his life for Muhammad, the Prophet of Islam, if he had to, because the Prophet was a human being whose way of life was inspiring. Mushafi found Muhammad an extremely rational being and concluded that reason was unique to the human race. He felt it would be a pity if human beings did not apply rationality in matters of life. To those who cared for him, his daredevil attitude sounded like a denial of the existence of God, and of religion. They feared for his safety, and attacks upon him by fanatics. They tried to silence him when he told his audience how he had travelled once farther than the caravan of human tears. He was in search of non-space when suddenly an angel called out to him and asked, 'Young man, what are you doing here wandering from place to place?' Mushafi replied that he was looking for the house of the maker of all creatures everywhere on earth. He was finally told to go to the heights of heaven. He used all the bravery in him to reach there, but his heart was not sure if he had reached his true goal. Was this the dwelling place that he had looked for? Now he had wandered in search of non-space. The angel told him that he understood nothing and in vain had he looked for the maker of all creatures in non-space. A space without a beginning or end like a room is a confined space within four walls. 'Return to the world of the living to find the abode of God who does not dwell in non-space,' the angel had said, dismissing the poet.

Mushafi is a favourite poet of Urdu critic Shamsur Rahman Faruqi. Mushafi wrote so much, but nineteenth-century critics did not find him original. Mushafi would have been forgotten if his work was not discovered in the twentieth century. In the 1990s and first decade of the 2000s, the writings of Mushafi were resurrected by publishers.

Till very recently, people were not aware of Mushafi and he was hardly read. But Faruqi was hungry to know about his past, where he came from, and where his literary perceptions fit in the larger picture. Faruqi's search led him to Mushafi and the critic found in the poet a kindred spirit. Faruqi discovered that he shared with Mushafi similar free ideas about God and religion. He loved Mushafi also for being so confident about his literary talent.

Mushafi marvels at the pride with which he steps on to the earth, making angels hail him in the heavens.

Rakhta hai kadam naaz se jis dum tu zameen par
Kehte hain farishte tujhe jai arsh-e-bareen par

Mushafi refused to box his view of the world into binaries. He valued spirituality as much as sensuality. There seemed no disagreements between the inner self and the outer, the personal and social, family and community, and spiritual and the material. He was able to combine spiritual longing with social concerns and with a desire for pleasure, joy, even erotica.

Having a young boy or two as a lover was part of life in that era. Mushafi's sensuous and erotic imageries in his writing betray that the poet may have engaged in more than one love affair at the same time.

Talking of himself Mushafi says that he did not miss out on a single lad and that he was quite a master at his calling, although, he adds, he is not much of a lover of boys despite the pleasure the beardless brats give him. He enjoyed intimacy with women and found the pleasure of love in women alone.

Poems written on unusual themes like this one may not necessarily be examples of self-experience but often an exercise in experimenting with fresh themes to write about, besides glorifying beauty and lamenting over separation from the beloved.

Mushafi is perhaps the last of the masters reflecting the classical style of Urdu poetry that developed in Delhi. Although born in Amroha district, Mushafi had studied in Delhi where he was first noticed as a budding poet. He migrated to Lucknow in the last quarter of the eighteenth century. This period is the beginning of a new way of *khayal bandi*, of contemplating upon life and expressing that view of life in a different way in verse. The beloved without whom joy is halved remained the centre of attention of the poet. Apart from this central theme of desire and praise of the beloved, the poet inspired the audience with words that were entertaining but also begging the listener to speculate and to philosophise a little more.

Mushafi points out that regimes have a different meaning—after all, the rooster too wears a crown on its head:

Saltanat aur bhi maane rakhti hain
Yun toh sar par khurus ke bhi hai taj

Poets like Mushafi were champions of this fresh form of creativity. Mushafi was happy to change his style of thought in the footsteps of Aatish. So what if Aatish was a student of Mushafi? Mushafi admired Aatish for sprinkling his writing with deep spirituality. Aatish was a role model also because he wrote the way he had lived. He was a humble faqir and his words were devoid of sensuality. He wrote in the free-flowing language of ordinary people that connected him to many more listeners. Inspired by Aatish, Mushafi had tried to elevate his physical world to the spiritual and to feel at home in both.

On the other hand, Nasikh was strict about the use of language. He was a serious scholar and he concentrated on formalising the grammar of the Urdu language, using Persian as a template. Due to their different approach to poetry, two camps of admirers had emerged in the city: one swore by the talent of Nasikh, and the other adored the work of the unselfconscious Aatish.

As far as Mushafi was concerned, he was fair to all talent. He had feared neither man nor God and was respectful towards creation. His writing reveals him to be extremely open-minded, and believing in the unity of all religions. Mushafi was convinced that all human beings and their beliefs come from a single source. He sounded like a mystic, but he was no Sufi either.

In his youth, Mushafi was least interested in learning. He spent his time flying kites, playing marbles and looking at young girls of the neighbourhood. While still tender of age, he was mocked by a woman in Amroha. Mushafi was infatuated with this woman and she admitted to him that yes, she was attracted to him too. She had desired him but she did not see a future with him. The object of Mushafi's desire had dismissed him with a cruel taunt that surely Mushafi did not expect her to spend the rest of her life living on poetry, did he? And if he did not, then he should return to her only after he had made a man of himself. This rebuke from one whose dust he wore like a robe over his fragile feelings destroyed his spirit for a moment. Mushafi had left home soon after and lived in many cities trying to make money.

He had packed a modest bag and bid Amroha, his place of birth, goodbye and taken to the road in search of manhood. His soul soaked in sorrow, Mushafi had sobbed all the way at the thought that his heart had refused to travel with him. However, the romantic temperament of Mushafi obviously did not enjoy a vacuum.

The young man arrived in Delhi and fell madly in love all over again. His heart had returned to him but only to turn to clay in Delhi like in the hands of a potter. His eyes did not stop raining tears of blood as the beauty who bewitched him, this time, refused to notice his presence. Her indifference struck him like a butcher's knife that minced his heart into meat. Any thought of her that crossed his mind made his head throb. He felt like he had been struck by a thousand storms, like he was being thrashed by repeated flashes of lightning. He was scared that perhaps it was his destiny to drown in his own tears.

He wrote poetry furiously and all the time, composing verses even as he talked. Mushafi noticed that if he was found crying, the irate beloved would ask him to take his tearful eyes somewhere else.

Saamne uske lagun rone toh jhunjhlaake kahe
Yahaan se le jaiye yeh deeda-e-tar aur kahin

Once he took his verses for Mirza Sauda to see. He was politely welcomed by the master poet who was preoccupied with his dogs. Sauda was extremely courteous for a few minutes and then he went back to combing the silken coat of his long-haired dogs. Mushafi was uncomfortable, and after lingering a while, he left Sauda with a sinking feeling. On his way home he burst into laughter at the thought of Sauda playing with his dogs. He related the incident to his companions. Mushafi's brilliant pupil Nurul Islam Muntazir was not amused and mocked the senior poet in a biting satire on Sauda, that has since been lost.

There were other satires composed by Mushafi and his pupils during his war with fellow poet Insha Allah Khan. All these satires were destroyed soon after they were written. Being the gentleman that Mushafi was, he was not fond of satires and felt uneasy using words to hurt other human beings. Much later in life, and after many a dalliance, Mushafi realised that he was wedded to knowledge.

The one woman who was eventually able to appreciate Mushafi's love for books, wisdom and wit ended up as his wife. The couple spent three decades of their life together. His beloved had enjoyed setting up a modest home for him and did not resent Mushafi for being indifferent towards money. She had giggled when he teased her and said that he was rich with the wealth of poetry and that gold and silver had little value for Mushafi.

Born in Amroha, Uttar Pradesh, in 1747, Mushafi lived in many cities, trying to earn a living before he arrived in Lucknow at the palatial home of the affluent Kanji Mal Saba, a leading silver merchant, a Persian poet and ardent admirer of Mushafi. The silver merchant lived in Khayaliganj not far from the Akbari Gate in the Chowk area of Lucknow. The Khatri Baniya Vaishnavi was a great admirer of Mushafi and invited him to stay as a house guest for as long as he liked.

Mushafi had many students but Saba was one of his prominent pupils. Mushafi had corrected Saba's writing and shared with him a love for the finer points of Persian poetry. Mushafi is remembered as a delightful conversationalist who composed verses as he spoke, enchanting people with his words and his many acts of generosity. Unmarried at that time, Mushafi treated Saba's wife like a daughter-in-law.

His imaginative vitality earned him many students and a colossal reputation. Writing in Lucknow in late eighteenth century, it is Mushafi who first called the language he used Urdu. He prayed that God preserve the language that he had first heard Mir Taqi Mir and Mirza Sauda speak, and which belongs to all of us now.

Khuda rakhe zubaan humne suni hai 'Mir' o 'Mirza' ki
Kahein kisi munh se hum, ae 'Mushafi', Urdu humaari hai

Remember how Khan Arzu had said to Sauda that Persian was not his mother tongue. That Sauda's poetry would be worthy of even greater praise if he wrote in the words of native speakers. If he were to compose in Urdu, his verses would be unique. Arzu had pointed out the absurdity of writing in one language, and speaking in another.

Sauda took the advice of the older poet who was also his mentor. He began to write in Urdu, inspiring younger poets to do the same. The mushaira was in existence since the sixteenth century, and the tradition was to recite in Persian at the regular gathering of poets.

It was Khan Arzu who got his students to use local imagery and vocabulary from the local Avadhi dialect in their writing.

Mushafi was nine years old when Khan Arzu died, but he was guided by Sauda, and inspired by Mir Taqi Mir, to write in Urdu. When he was mature enough to do so, Mushafi had put his tongue in his cheek and wrote that the time of Mir and Mirza Sauda was over and that it was now the age of Mushafi to lay down the rules.

Over time, Mushafi stopped using Arabic and Persian words in his writing. He told his many students that Arabic and Persian vocabulary was no sacred cow and that enchanting poetry could still be written in a language more intimate with the self. He was a voracious reader and would walk anywhere, for miles if he had to, to trace a book that was unavailable close to him. If it was the only copy, Mushafi would painstakingly copy down each word by hand from the precious book so that it was available to him whenever he wanted to read it. Poetry was his passion and for Mushafi there was no poetry without knowledge. Along with poetry, his other love was beauty. It was wit that allowed him to cope with the unpleasantness in life, and he was gifted with a marvellous sense of humour.

He wrote that his hands had remained empty in life and if his talent was talked about in golden words after his death, so what?

If Mushafi disliked anyone with all his heart, it was the Europeans living in Lucknow. He had nothing personal against the English but resented their intrusion in Avadh. He found the military manoeuvrings of the officials of the British East India Company hateful. Even the scholarly work taken up by the British was seen by Mushafi as a colonial project to control, exploit and steal the riches of this land. The scholarship by the British was spoilt by prejudices both cultural and racial that distorted the values of the way of life here. The arrogance and pride of the British was unbearable to him and he had little time for their belief in their superiority in every way over Indians.

He doubted if the British could ever be fair in love or war. In the battle in Bengal, the British had bribed the opponent's commander-in-chief to defect, and to join their side of the battle. Mushafi recalled the way Colonel Robert Clive, first British Governor of the Bengal Presidency, had bribed Mir Jafar, commander-in-chief of the Bengal army. Clive had promised to make Mir Jafar the Nawab of Bengal. That is how Clive was able to defeat Nawab Siraj-ud-Daula, ruler of Bengal, at Plassey in 1757 with the help of the Mir Jafar.

At the turn of the eighteenth century, many Europeans had lived in Lucknow. Many of them had enjoyed Urdu poetry, and hosted a mushaira. Sauda wrote a qasida for Richard Johnson, chief assistant of the Resident of Lucknow, and dedicated his first collection of poems to Johnson.

Meanwhile John Gilchrist, a medical doctor with the British East India Company, began to study Hindustani. On his tours around the Avadh region, he realised that everyone spoke Hindustani in the countryside. He could communicate with the people in Hindustani, but not in Persian.

Gilchrist left the medical services to study Hindustani, and to publish *A Dictionary: English and Hindoostanee* in 1790. At Gilchrist's suggestion, the East India Company started the Oriental Seminary or Gilchrist *ka* madrasa, to give practical lessons in Hindustani for administrative purposes to British officers in Calcutta. Within a year, the madrasa graduated into the formidable Fort William College and became a centre for Urdu prose. At Fort Williams, the linguist had no time for poetry. He wanted to get on with the practical business of making the local people believe that the presence of the British in their midst was no less than a miracle. The Fort Williams College translated the New Testament of the Bible into Persian, Urdu and Hindi.

By the early nineteenth century, the British had replaced Persian with the Urdu language in the bureaucracy. Gilchrist also introduced studies of Hindi language and literature, and commissioned a Hindi translation of the Bible along with *Udant Martand*, the first Indian Hindi language newspaper in 1826. Gilchrist is responsible for the bifurcation of the vernacular language of the khadi boli into two languages of Hindi and Urdu, each with its own script. Gilchrist was a great lover of Urdu, but he also encouraged a more formal form of khadi boli and called it Hindi.

The behaviour of officials of the British East India Company had become increasingly obnoxious. Around the mid-eighteenth century, high-handedness had reached epic proportions. The Company refused to pay taxes to Bengal. It befriended, protected and took under its wing all those like Mir Jafar who were critical of the ruler. The Company tried its best to grab land that was leased to it in Calcutta for trade purposes. After the defeat of Bengal by Robert Clive at Plassey, the Battle of Buxar followed in 1764. Shuja-ud-Daula, ruler of Avadh, joined the battle along with the forces of Delhi's Mughal emperor and the Bengal ruler. Yet another defeat for the Indians at Buxar broke the back of Shuja-ud-Daula's army and facilitated direct control of the Gangetic plains to the British.

After Buxar, Shuja-ud-Daula did not fight another big battle. Till his death in 1775, he spent the remaining decade of his life building Faizabad into a splendid capital city where literary activities, especially poetry recitation, was a favourite pastime.

In *Awadh under the Nawabs: Politics, Culture and Communal Relations 1722–1856*, author Surendra Mohan writes:

> During his lifetime Faizabad and Lucknow had a parallel growth. Faizabad was the capital town, and Lucknow was the center of commercial activities, arts, culture and learning. Geographically, Lucknow was the centre for trade between the Doab and the area east of River Gomti. At the confluence in Prayagraj, the River Ganga and the River Jamuna meet. Here geography and history come together, and in that confluence, there evolved a new culture which may justly be called the Ganga–Jamuni *tehzeeb*, or way of life. With the decline of Delhi, Lucknow rose in eminence in all fields of activity.

Shuja-ud-Daula lost one-third of the revenue of his territory to the British after the defeat at Buxar. In return, the British guaranteed Avadh's security and its independence from Delhi. With a strong military presence and the posting of a British representative to keep an eye on military and administrative affairs, Shuja-ud-Daula was free from Mughal domination and also available to spend time with poets who were spilling over at his court. He moved to Faizabad to splurge on building a new capital city, one that could rival Delhi.

Shuja-ud-Daula welcomed merchants from Persia, China and Europe. He was fond of music, dance and musicians.

Courtesans, dancers, singers and instrumentalists benefited from Shuja-ud-Daula's generous patronage. Shuja-ud-Daula decided to spend his wealth on his people before the British robbed him of everything. Once Shuja-ud-Daula settled down to live in Faizabad, crowds flocked to the city.

In no time, people of every social and religious background, and individuals of every rank and class, had made Faizabad their home. During the reign of Shuja-ud-Daula, the madrasa (traditional schools of learning) in Faizabad acquired great fame and attracted a large number of teachers and students from all over the Indian subcontinent. However, Faizabad fell into disrepair once Shuja-ud-Daula's son and successor Asaf-ud-Daula moved the capital to Lucknow where many Mughal princes followed him, including Mirza Ilahi Baksh, Mirza Husain Baksh and Mirza Sulaiman Shikoh, the third son of Shah Alam II, the emperor of Delhi.

Sulaiman was a poet and he hosted many poets in his Lucknow home by the riverbank. Fearing for his life in the lawless lanes of Delhi, Sulaiman had fled Delhi in 1790 and lived in Lucknow as a guest of the rulers of Avadh till 1828. Although a refugee, Sulaiman maintained a lavish lifestyle and offered patronage to hundreds of poets and artists who came to Lucknow from all over north India.

According to Urdu critic Ali Jawad Zaidi, at least sixty-five poets had migrated around this time from Delhi to Lucknow. Sulaiman maintained an envious collection of books in his library including the diwans of Mushafi. The library in Rampur still has many books embossed with the seal of Sulaiman.

After Shuja-ud-Daula, Asaf-ud-Daula and Saadat Ali Khan, Sulaiman was the fourth most important patron of poets in Lucknow. Mushafi too found employment at the court of Sulaiman where his job was to correct the already lightweight verses of the poet prince. Sulaiman wrote that the beloved should not tarry like the others but should take him in her embrace:

Auron ki tarah se ab na taalo
Humko apne gale laga lo

In another couplet, the poet prince advises himself to cross over from the path of idol worship to the path of God:

Buth-khaane ki raah ko Sulaiman chhodo tum
Aur raah-e-khuda lo

One day Insha Allah Khan, another poet from Delhi, arrived at the court of Sulaiman. Insha was already well known. He was a clever poet and he came to Lucknow to make a living, like so many other poets before him, including Mushafi. Born in Murshidabad in West Bengal in 1752, the flamboyant Insha humoured the Mughal prince in exile to such an extent that he was loath to have Insha out of his sight. Sulaiman could not have enough of the fireworks of jest that Insha cracked without a break. He livened up a meet with his presence as he went around offering courtesies in one direction and making funny faces in the opposite direction. His behaviour was sometimes gentlemanly, and sometimes that of a jester and a rake. One day Insha appeared with his beard shaved on one side and on another day with a shaved head, beard and eyebrows.

Two years older than the prince, and more than three decades younger to Mushafi, Insha impressed one and all with his dynamic personality, his mastery over poetry and the languages, and endless talent for buffoonery. Insha's presence at court and at public places provided much laughter and comic relief. All this while, Urdu poetry had been devoid of humour and satire. So those looking for sheer entertainment at the gathering of poets were delighted to have Insha in their midst. Insha was also his own admirer number one. He bragged about his talents and good looks, and could not get audiences to shower enough praise upon him.

Mushafi thought the younger poet was talented and brilliant, but did not think that Insha was solid in his learning, or stable in his behaviour. To bask in non-stop praise from the audience was something Mushafi found distasteful. However, every time Mushafi heard Insha recite verses that touched his heart, he would put away his own verse. He would acknowledge that what he had heard from Insha was so good that nothing else recited after that could sound better.

Sulaiman began to spend more time with Insha. He chose Insha to correct his verses. Mushafi's responsibilities at Sulaiman's court were reduced, and so was his salary. A rivalry developed between Mushafi and Insha. Instead of stepping in to mediate between the two poets in a mature manner, Sulaiman found it more entertaining to watch them bicker. Both were encouraged by Sulaiman to insult each other in verse. This inspired the young disciples of both the poets to engage in a war of words with each other. Once Mushafi's disciples got together and marched to Insha's home to lampoon him. The clever Insha welcomed the group and listened to what they wanted to recite. He praised the youngsters and entertained them with food and drinks. He played the jester before the protestors and made them laugh with his silliness.

After he saw them off, he sat down to plot revenge. Insha planned a public procession like a wedding that was led by puppeteers holding two puppets. The puppet in one hand was dressed like a bride, while the one in the other hand was the groom. The procession paraded through the main streets of Lucknow, reciting hurtful satires and showing the puppets fighting with each other. Mushafi was ridiculed to the beat of drums and to a chorus that sang of a new play under the ancient sky about the quarrels between the groom Mushafi and his bride, the *mushafin*.

The episode was in bad taste. The verses composed by Insha were funny, but lewd. The elderly Mushafi endured the insults with dignity. He was hurt that in this war of words, Sulaiman had encouraged Insha and lauded his bad behaviour. Mushafi voiced his anguish in verse saying that he had no recourse but to depart from the door of Sulaiman as there was no humanity or honour left there. C.M. Naim and Carla Petievich write in *Lucknow: Memories of a City* (edited by Violett Graff) that within the context of patrons and poets, one prominent feature of the literary milieu that emerged in Lucknow was a furious public display of rivalry between poets.

> Rivalry among poets was always a prominent feature of literary life in the pre-modern days. Its causes lay in the institutions of mushaira—etymologically, the word implies contestation and courtly patronage... In Lucknow, in contrast to Delhi and the Deccan, we find such rivalry taking on the proportions of processions and street fights.

Both poets and their respective patrons were only following an age-old tradition of displaying personal rivalries on the streets in Lucknow. People were already used to this kind of public entertainment and thoroughly enjoyed different kinds of contests, fights or *ladaai*, like kite flying, cock fights, quail fights and regular mock performances of abusive quarrels between working-class women.

Yet, when Insha died, Mushafi's generosity of nature made him write in wonder if he had anything left in his life to enjoy after Insha's death.

Khvaab thha ya khayaal thha kya thha
Hijr thha ya visaal thha kya thha
Mere pehlu mein raat jaag-kar vo
Maah thha ya hilaal thha kya thha
Chamki bijli si par na samjhe hum
Husn thha ya jamaal thha kya thha
Shab jo dil do do haath uchhalta thha
Vajd thha ya voh haal thha kya thha
Jisko hum roz-e-hijr samjhe thhe
Maah thha ya voh saal thha kya thha
'Mushafi' shab jo chup tu baitha thha
Kya tujhe kuchh malaal thha kya thha

Was it a dream or reverie, what was it?
Was it absence or presence, what was it?
The night spent in my arms
Was it the full moon or crescent, what was it?
Thunder-loud warnings I did not heed
Was it beauty was it goodness, what was it?
The evening when the heart skipped many a beat

Was it real or unreal, what was it?
What seemed like a daily loss
Was it month or year, what was it?
Mushafi, the evening you sat so quiet
Was it regret, what was it?

Log kehte hain mohabbat mein asar hota hai
Kaun se sheher mein hota hai kidhar hota hai
Usske kooche mein hai nit surat-e-bedaad nai
Qatl har khasta baa-andaaz-e-digar hota hai
Nahin maaloom ki maatam hai falaq par kiska
Roz kyun chaak girebaan-e-seher hota hai
Wahin yun hi apni bhi hai baareek-tar-az-mu gardan
Tegh ke saath yahan zikr-e-kamar hota hai
Karke main yaad dil apne ko bahut rota hun
Jab kisi shakhs ka duniya se safar hota hai
Uski mizhgaan ka koi naam na lo kya haasil
Mera in baaton se suraakh jigar hota hai
'Mushafi' hum toh tere milne ko aaye kayi baar
Ae deewane tu kisi vaqt bhi ghar hota hai

I am told that love is divine
In which place is it so, where is it so?
Every day I am abused in the beloved's home
Destroyed in different ways
Don't know who the heavens mourn
And who tatters dawn every morn
The neck is placed in a position delicate

I wish all talk of the sword around the waist did sit
Thought of my heart makes me bawl
When the worldly journey of a human being has a fall
Mention not her eyelashes, what is the use?
Such talk ruptures the soul like abuse
'Mushafi' I came to see you often
When are you ever home, you crazy person?

FOUR

Nasikh and Aatish

Shaikh Imam Baksh Nasikh and Khwaja Haider Ali Aatish were two of Mushafi's favourite students and the closest people to him in Lucknow. Their popularity was at its peak at the turn of the eighteenth century.

The coronation of Ghazi-ud-Din Haider Shah as the first king of Avadh, and the last *naib* of the Mughals in 1814, freed the rulers of Avadh of its economic, political and linguistic domination by Delhi. This freedom cost the Avadh treasury one and a half crore rupees paid to the British for supporting Avadh's independence.

Ghazi-ud-Din Haider's father Saadat Ali Khan had already surrendered half the kingdom of Avadh to the British for their help in his succession to the throne of Lucknow. Ghazi-ud-Din, now king and formerly vassal of the Mughal emperor, was encouraged by the British to defy the Mughal emperor and to assume the title of king offered to him by the British. The noose of the British was tightening around Avadh. The British saw themselves getting stronger. Nasikh disapproved of the rulers of Avadh who had betrayed Delhi when the Mughal rule was at its weakest to help the British.

One day Ghazi-ud-Din sent a messenger to Nasikh asking him to come to his court as he wanted Nasikh to recite an ode in his praise. In return, Ghazi-ud-Din promised to confer upon Nasikh the title of Poet Laureate. When Ghazi-ud-Din's minister, who was also a student of Nasikh, brought the royal message to the poet, Nasikh expressed annoyance. He said if Mirza Sulaiman Shikoh, Mughal prince in Lucknow, should become king, he would accept a title from him. Or the English government could bestow titles. But a title from Ghazi-ud-Din? Of what use would that title be to him?

When Ghazi-ud-Din heard Nasikh's response to his offer, he was angry and immediately exiled Nasikh from Lucknow. Nasikh lived in different places for a while, but after Ghazi-ud-Din's death in 1827, he returned to Lucknow.

Ghazi-ud-Din had set up the first letter press in Lucknow, which printed beautiful books that reached many readers.

The Urdu language in Lucknow was free of the strict rules that were followed in Delhi. During the lifetime of Mushafi, Nasikh and Aatish, the language to usher in a golden age of poetry writing had arrived. It was impossible to stop the citizens of Lucknow from speaking the way they wanted to, and who insisted that their language was an authority in its own right. They let the people in Delhi say *andhyari*, referring to the same dark night as *andheri raat*. Without worrying about what Delhi would say, the cream in the milk continued to be called *balai* in Lucknow instead of *malai*. Tobacco remained *tamaku* while tobacco that went inside betel leaves was *tambaku*. There was no need any more to say tobacco is tambaku and tobacco in betel leaves is *zarda* in imitation of Delhi.

At first, most of the mentors of poets in Lucknow were from Delhi. But with master teachers like Nasikh, the fountainhead of poetic practices and inspiration could be found in Lucknow itself. Idioms used in Delhi were no longer considered the only source of pride. Nasikh's use of words and idioms was perfect. He was a guru most revered in Lucknow and everyone thought it an honour to learn from Nasikh.

The word Urdu was in common use. All lyrical verses and poems of love called rekhta in the past were now known as ghazal. The students of Nasikh and Aatish avoided the unnecessary use of Arabic and Persian vocabulary in their writing. The Persian style descriptions of the physical beauty of the beloved, and exaggerated praise of the dark, twisted and thick curls of her tresses were also avoided. Younger poets were encouraged to look for more creative themes or *mauzu*, and to find inspiration in local similes and metaphors instead of monotonous references to doves, nightingales, wine and the tavern found in decadent Persian poetry. The licence to poets to use colloquial speech also led to many a mediocre composition that was hawked as poetry.

Like a complaint by Saadat Yaar Khan Rangin who asks the crazy one to come to him as wretched sleep is nowhere in sight. Says the poet, come, and tales of what you have been up to today for me recite.

Neend aati nahin kambakht divaani aaja
Apni beeti koi keh aaj kahaani aaja

The best poetry remains that which is able to combine the

loftiness of imagination and feelings with the strength of thought. Notes Imam Baksh Nasikh that in advanced years his heart is black and the hair white like a house that is dark inside but lit up by moonlight outside.

Dil siyaah hai baal hain sab apne peeri mein safed
Ghar ke andar hai andhera aur baahar chandni

Nasikh was wealthy, knowledgeable and welcomed everywhere by everyone. People were flattered to host him in their home. On his exile from Lucknow by Ghazi-ud-Din, Nasikh went to Allahabad and spent time with a group of mystics. Raja Chandu Lal, chief minister of Hyderabad, sent him twelve thousand rupees so that he could visit him in Hyderabad. Nasikh wrote back saying that if he went anywhere from Allahabad, it would be to Lucknow. The Raja sent an additional fifteen thousand rupees, promising Nasikh the title of Chief Poet. He added that Nasikh was not expected to play courtier. He could come and go to court as he pleased.

Nasikh did not accept the offer and distributed the money that came to him from Hyderabad amongst the poor. It was Nasikh's habit to spend lavishly on himself but he also gave money to those in need. He helped pilgrims who wanted to visit Mecca for Haj, and those without home or hearth. Nasikh had the money and time to journey from Faizabad to Lucknow, Allahabad, Varanasi and Patna. In Allahabad, he enjoyed the company of wise men and mystics.

Wrote Nasikh that wherever he may travel, his feet always turn around and take him back to the mystics. He liked Varanasi and wanted to live there but he got lonely after a few days. He said that he did not find anyone he liked in the city. In Patna he was treated like royalty but he left saying that his language was in danger of being ruined in that city.

Urdu literary life in Avadh had come into its own. It had been lit up by poets and scholars who came from Delhi following attacks on the city by Iranian, Afghan, Maratha and Jat armies. Lucknow had welcomed the immigrants and now that Avadh was independent of Delhi, it continued to offer generous patronage to poets, writers and scholars of Urdu and Persian.

Nasikh did not need a patron, or payment for writing poetry. He had inherited enough riches and could afford to spend all his time at home, being his own master. His father was Khuda Baksh, an affluent tent maker. It is suspected that the wealthy businessman had no children so he had adopted Nasikh, the son of a poor man, in Faizabad. Nasikh received the best education possible in Lucknow and was never denied comfort in his childhood. However, when the merchant died, his brothers appeared to contest his fortune. An uncle even tried to allegedly poison Nasikh. But thanks to his friend who was a djinn, a spirit who was invisible to the world, Nasikh was warned early enough about the poison that was added to his meal of bread made from gram flour and mashed in clarified butter.

The djinn had advised Nasikh to invite some friends as witnesses. In front of the friends, the first morsel of the meal prepared for him was to be fed to a dog. That way the whole world was witness to the dog's death after he had swallowed the food given to him. The family quarrel was taken to court. The argument of Nasikh's uncles was malicious. They wanted to disinherit him because they said Nasikh was an adopted son and a slave. Nasikh poured his pain into poetry crying how false the blame of his uncles was. His father had treated him like his own child and that is why he had left his worldly possessions to Nasikh. Besides, if it is true that he was adopted then was it a sin to be adopted? Is fate not capricious? Poverty and wealth change hands like the seasons. One day the wheel of fortune may favour a poor man with a windfall, making him the richest overnight. The next day fate could deliver misfortune to the rich depriving him of everything that he ever owned, argued Nasikh. In the end, the court voted in favour of Nasikh.

In Lucknow, Nasikh's teacher in Arabic and Persian was Waris Ali Lakhnavi and he studied the texts prescribed at the Firangi Mahal school in the same neighbourhood where he lived. Nasikh never married because women did not interest him. He lived alone in a house in the oldest part of Lucknow, the Chowk. The house is no longer there. It was probably in one of the lanes of the Taksaali Mohalla, in the neighbourhood of the main mint factory that does not exist anymore. Nasikh died in 1838 and was buried in the same place, although it is not possible to trace his grave today.

He had entertained many visitors, and students came in droves to show him their work till noon. At that hour Nasikh was found sitting on the carpet, resting against a bolster and surrounded by students. Most of his students were sons from well-to-do families and these children of the city's nobility held their breath in the presence of Nasikh out of love and respect for the poet. Nasikh was forever writing, and he was often lost in thought. He had little to say to most visitors. He was happiest in the company of the djinn.

Once, a visitor was reluctant to leave. He kept sitting with Nasikh even though the poet had stopped speaking with him. When several hours had passed by, Nasikh beckoned to one of his servants and asked him to bring him a particular box. He opened the box and took out the deed of his home and handed the papers to the visitor, saying, 'Since you have overstayed your visit, you might like to stay here forever.'

To another, upon being requested to explain a verse in the Persian language, he said, 'I am not a Persian poet.'

Nasikh was not witty, and he was better known for his reserve rather than his humour. He was very particular about the form of poetry. In fact, he concentrated so much on craft that spontaneity often escaped his writing. Nasikh wrote poetry not to entertain but to prick the conscience of the reader, and therefore it is devoid of diversion and laughter.

Nasikh wants the wine-giver to hurry before it is too late and clouds sail back and forth threateningly.

Aati jaati hai jaa-ba-jaa badli
Saaqiya jald aa havaa badli

Nasikh was hardworking despite being wealthy. He was disciplined and strict. His contribution in streamlining rekhta, a language born out of a mixture of languages and local dialects, is incredible, but often Nasikh the prude and the puritan got the better of Nasikh the poet, depriving his writing of emotions and deeper feelings.

Nasikh is emotional when he says that it is not possible for him to suddenly give up thoughts of her tresses as he has nursed the dark cobra for so long. But perhaps the emotion lacks depth?

Kis tarah chhod dun yakayak teri zulfon ka khayaal
Ek muddat se yeh kaale naag hain paale hue

Everyone was aware that they must beg leave of Nasikh at noon. It was whispered that the djinn who was in love with Nasikh would visit him at that hour. There were attendants who reported sounds that they heard as if Nasikh was not alone in the room locked by him from inside. But no one dared to question Nasikh who looked more like a butcher than a poet. He was very tall, with a broad physique and a sunless, dark complexion. Because of his dark look, he was called a buffalo without a tail. Nasikh sensed what was said about him behind his back and he replied to all those who tried to torment him in verse. He said that to look at, he may not be equal to the beauty of the moon, but he was grateful that he was not black inside.

He kept his beard and his head shaved, and his bald pate was always well oiled. The only hair visible on his face was that of an impressive moustache, trimmed dramatically to match the mystery in his eyes. Even in the cold of the winter months, Nasikh wore a loose tunic in thick cotton and in a bright red colour that he wrapped around his waist like all other wrestlers. Around his neck hung a necklace with a heavy pendant of a precious stone. The staff that he carried in his hand had a silver head, and there was a metallic ring around the handle for a better grip over the weapon. He ate only one meal a day that was worth several kilos of the finest food, making some suspect that the djinn resided in Nasikh's stomach. During the mango season he made a meal of several basketfuls of only that king of fruits. In the same way he would enjoy a meal of the seasonal corn on the cob in countless quantity, and nothing else. He would skin the cob and roast it on coal, bathing it in lemon juice, salt and ground black pepper. He relished the taste of each dish separately, saying that if different delicacies are mixed up then it is impossible to enjoy the pleasure of eating. Nasikh preferred to dine alone and visitors would leave when it was time for him to eat.

Apart from poetry, his other passion was intensive physical exercise. Each day he would wake up three hours before dawn to exercise. Every day he did push-ups, and when he exposed himself to the world in little except a loincloth, he looked like a lion about to spring at his prey. After a bath he would sit on a cane chair in the courtyard that was swept spotlessly clean for him, and strewn with low stools for visitors. The inside of his room was carpeted where he welcomed his students in the morning. The work of all the students was collected in a large bag by his caretaker and given to him for correction. He would discuss poetry with the students, asking them to read out the verses they had written. After carefully listening to each student, he would either give his okay to their work, dismiss it, or make necessary changes. This exercise is part of the master–pupil institution of learning as practised for ages in north India and it does not exist in any other tradition of ghazal writing, including the Indo-Persian. The apprenticeship system was perfected over time as an invaluable process of personal interaction between mentor and pupil. The aim was to improve the poetry of the younger poets. It was usual for the master to change a word or two so that the two lines were able to better connect the thought with feelings.

After the visitors and students had left, Nasikh would

enjoy his only meal of the day, in the company of his friend, the djinn. Nasikh said that he ordered large meals because he shared them with the djinn. On the rooftop of his home there was a room where Nasikh would escape from the world to rest after a meal. A few hours of sleep later, Nasikh would wake up to treat himself to long, deep puffs from the hookah, or the hubble bubble, which he loved to prepare with tobacco flavoured with a variety of exotic aromas. The earthen bowl of the hookah was filled with burning coal, and tobacco was spread over the fire. Each puff of tobacco was inhaled through a tube painted in colourful patterns and connected to water gurgling in a container at the base of the hookah. Nasikh had a great collection of hookahs. Out of the roomful of hookahs some had been bought by him, while others had come to him as gifts from admirers and friends.

Nasikh had each hookah fitted with different tubes covered in a coat of silk and patterns woven in gold and silver thread. Whenever he hosted a formal get-together, Nasikh would prepare one hookah for each guest and top it with their favourite tobacco. Even on these occasions, the process of correcting the verses of his students would continue from behind a thick wall of sweet-smelling smoke rising from the many hookahs that were smoked without pause.

Every day Nasikh would sort out the poetry left in the large bag by his students. He would spend time reading and correcting the work of his students after his afternoon nap. Once night was at its darkest and the world had slipped into silence, then Nasikh would take out his pen and dip it, as if in the blood of his heart, to string words into such clever poetry that none other was able to write.

Jis qadar hum se tum hue nazdeek
Uss qadar duur kar diya humko

The way you got close to me—the same way I was distanced from you.

Since Nasikh wrote poetry for the love of it and not for money, he was not desperate to impress anyone or to attract attention to his work with recitals at public places. His style was to write and to put the writing away for a while. He would read it a couple of days later and correct it himself, never reciting it to another. He followed this practice till he was confident that it was exactly what he wanted to say. Only then did he feel ready to recite at a mushaira.

Nasikh attended the public gathering of poets out of curiosity. He liked listening to other poets. For years he did not feel the need to recite at a mushaira. But sitting at a mushaira, listening to great poetry recited by his elders, made his heart flutter. He enjoyed the idea of learning, and his affluence and knowledge attracted the learned and the accomplished to his home. In their company, Nasikh's ideas and words received natural correction.

At the home of Mirza Haji Sahab, Qalandar Baksh Jurat, Mirza Muhammad Hasan Qatil, Insha, Mushafi and others would gather to recite. Nasikh would also be there, but to listen. He was too shy to recite at first. He would sit quietly and enjoy listening to the poetry, especially of Insha and Jurat whose verses were peppered with salt and spice, which was often missing from the recitation of other poets. Gradually, ambition blossomed in the heart of Nasikh and one day he woke up to find that he was ready to recite at the next mushaira.

> On that occasion Mirza Haji Sahab, Mirza Qatil and Haji Muhammad Sadiq Khan 'Akhtar' showed great appreciation, and through their encouragement my poetry began to go from strength to strength every day. And enthusiasm was born in people's hearts, so that they kept wanting more.

It was at a mushaira that Aatish first heard Nasikh recite his poetry. According to Nasikh, Aatish was consumed by envy. And in a fit of jealousy, Aatish had recited verses with such desperation that blood began to drip from his chest.

The admirers and students of Aatish immediately geared up to insult Nasikh. Those on the side of Aatish complained that Nasikh's work was full of sound and fury but was devoid of tenderness and feelings. That Nasikh was a master of words but the way he used words did not touch the heart. He brought sophistication and purity to the Urdu language but he was also abusive. Both the poets had used obscene vocabulary in public to hurt each other—to the delight of the audience. Nasikh and Aatish had many disciples who found it entertaining to watch the poets engage in a war of words. Mischief-makers made sure that loathing between the two poets escalated to such an extent that Nasikh and Aatish decided not to attend the same mushaira. Aatish always went to the mushaira hosted by the poet Nawab Sayyid Muhammad Khan Rind and Sahab Mirza Shinavar where he was showered with praise for his poetic use of simple language.

When Nasikh did not feel like participating in any mushaira, he would send verses to the gathering of poets for recitation on his behalf by one of his students. It was not uncommon to make an announcement at a mushaira requesting all gentlemen to be all ears to the ustad of ustads as the ghazal from Nasikh was recited. Hearing the message from Nasikh, silence would reign over the poets' gathering. After the recitation of Nasikh's work by his student, other poets would be invited to continue their recitation.

Nasikh and Aatish loved to tease each other when they happened to be at the same mushaira. Aatish had taunted Nasikh in verse wondering if he was aware of what people said about him behind his back. In certain recitations, the quick-tempered Aatish referred to Nasikh as an adopted child, mocking his wealth and his looks. While the audience cheered, Nasikh often sat in stoic silence.

At a rare mushaira, the guests were relieved that the evening had ended and the host was happy to see Nasikh and Aatish head towards their respective homes. The host was a great admirer of Nasikh and wanted to honour the poet at a mushaira organised by him. When the quick-tempered Aatish heard this, he was furious. Anger made him restless and he walked out of his home to aimlessly wander around in the thick forest near his home. He bit his fingernails and fidgeted with his long hair. He flung his long braid this way and that, making the cap parked on his head at an angle nearly fall. He found a place to sit on the steps of a mosque and composed a poem. He took that poem to the mushaira, along with the sword that he had pulled out of the sheath worn around his waist.

At the mushaira the visitors were surprised to see the very tall, thin and sweet-faced Aatish hurry up towards the assembly of poets, waving a naked sword in his hand. Aatish found a place to sit exactly opposite Nasikh and placed the sword beside him. He listened to Nasikh recite his poem and straightened his shoulders. Throughout the recitation he would pick up the sword and drop it, repeating the gesture repeatedly. That day, Aatish made a lot of people nervous. His host was anxious. What if Aatish used the sword to make a hole in his stomach? he worried. But once he was told why Aatish was excited, he immediately ordered another robe of honour and bestowed it on Aatish. This way both Aatish and Nasikh were felicitated at the same mushaira. Once the rituals of the evening were over, the host heaved a sigh of relief to see the poets leave.

Aatish was born in a family of mystics in Faizabad in 1777. As a young man, he had joined the police force and that brief experience as a policeman had added swagger to his gait. He was a fine swordsman and seldom forgot to wear his sword around the waist. His father died when he was very young. That incident had interrupted his formal education, leaving none to help him deal with the wild side of his temperament.

Although not a sufi, Aatish lived his life like a faqir. He was not bookish, but made his poetry perfect with practice. He was a spontaneous and natural poet who chose to live modestly without self-pity and uncalled-for melancholia. Patience and contentment were part of his nature, but sometimes anger erupted out of him like lava from a volcano. Aatish could have spent what he earned on himself but he chose to live like many poverty-stricken people around him. Out of the eighty rupees he received from the ruler of Lucknow, he gave fifteen rupees to his wife and the rest was routinely distributed amongst those who were even poorer than him.

Often there was nothing to cook in his home. When well-wishers and students brought him food, he accepted the gifts with gratitude, adding, 'All of you keep me so well-fed that my greedy soul has become fat.'

Nasikh and Aatish were good friends, but it was the rogues around them who, for their own entertainment, provoked the two to make a spectacle of their rivalry in public. At one mushaira, Aatish was as gracious as he was expected to be. Nasikh had walked in hours after most of the guests had left. He sat down and made small talk with those present for a while. Then Nasikh asked Aatish if the mushaira was over. Aatish stood up and saluted Nasikh saying, 'The master's place is vacant. Everyone longs to hear from you.'

Once Syed Muhammad Khan Rind, a student of Aatish, wanted to end his relationship with his mentor. He went to Nasikh asking him to be his teacher. Poet Mirza Muhammad Raza Barq had accompanied Rind to Nasikh's home. Nasikh listened to the visitors and said, 'Rind takes care of Aatish and showers him with gifts. If I take you as my student, all that give and take between you and Aatish will stop and who will be seen as the sinner, but me? I have no need for gifts from Rind. It is best if Rind continues to learn from Aatish.'

That was the kind of concern that Nasikh nursed for Aatish. Their personalities were the polar opposite and perhaps that is why they found each other attractive. In poetry, Nasikh was particular about form and diction while the Aatish's concern was content and feelings. It was not Aatish's style to rigidly follow man-made rules. He had concentrated on expressing everyday experiences of the human heart, in carefully chosen lyrical but everyday vocabulary.

Here the poet is unable to entertain any other idea except a vision of the beloved while the desire to see her has made him blind:

Kuchh nazar aata nahin usske tasavvur ke siva
Hasrat-e-deedaar ne aankhon ko andha kar diya

Aatish's lifestyle too was vastly different from that of Nasikh. His home was a modest mud hut with a thatched roof on an elevated part of the Chowk area in Saraa-e-Baale Khan. Aatish did not live too far away from where Nasikh lived in style. A jute mat was spread on the floor of his room where he sat with those who came to see him. This is also where Aatish slept after the visitors had left. Aatish was fond of opium. He kept a horse that was always fed even when Aatish had little to eat. Once Aatish had apologised to an affluent visitor for being unable to provide him with bolsters and a carpet to sit on like in Nasikh's home. But people's admiration for Aatish rested not on the worldly possessions that he did not have, but on the fire or *aatish* found in his poetry. It continues to illuminate the private world of each of his listeners.

Says Aatish that except for sorrow there is nothing to gain in the wasteland; you should be grateful for every moment of peace you experience:

Sivaye ranjh kuchh haasil nahin hai iss kharaabe mein
Ghanimat jaan jo araam tu-ne koi dam paaya

Aatish was five years younger than Nasikh. The two poets had bonded well despite the many verbal wars between them. Together Nasikh and Aatish are most representative of the Lucknow style of ghazal writing. The earlier poets were born and brought up in Delhi, having shifted to Lucknow as adults. However, Nasikh and Aatish belong to Avadh. They died in Lucknow after having expressed themselves in verse throughout their life in a language that was less Persianised. Nasikh's writing was practical and bookish, while Aatish has left a lyrical legacy considered precious to this day.

Aatish lived to see the Royal Translation Bureau installed in Lucknow in 1827. This was a major contribution made by the ruler Ghazi-ud-Din Haider to literary activities in the city. Avadh became the first Indian state to have its own translation bureau. The job of the bureau was to provide texts of modern, scientific subjects in the Urdu language. Soon the Matba-e-Sultani press was established in the city, which published books in Urdu translated from other languages by the bureau. The work of poets too got published and was circulated amongst a larger group of people.

Aatish was grief-stricken when Nasikh died almost a decade before him, and he stopped writing poetry from that day. Aatish was unable to compose verses after Nasikh's death because the pleasure of composing poetry, he said, was in listening and in reciting.

'When the person I enjoyed reciting to is no more, then it is not poetry that I will compose, but gibberish,' Aatish said, throwing down his pen forever.

Aatish

Buth-khaana todiye masjid ko dhaaiye
Dil ko na todiye yeh khuda ka maqaam hai

Ajab teri hai ae yeh mehboob soorat
Nazar se gir gaye sab khoobsoorat
Ae sanam jisne tujhe chaand si soorat di hai
Ussi Allah ne mujhko bhi mohabbat di hai
Naapaak hoga kabhi husn-o-ishq ka jhagda
Vo kissa hai yeh ki jiska koi gavaah nahin
Sunn toh sahi jahaan mein hai tera fasaana kya
Kehti hai tujhko khalq-e-khuda gaa-ibaana kya

Tear down the temple, demolish the mosque
Break not the heart, home of the beloved
Extraordinary is the lover's beauty
All other loveliness pales away in front of it
The one who gave you moon-like beauty
The same creator gave me love
Favour not feud between beauty and love
It is an experience without witness
Listen to the legends spread about you
The world believes that you are not you.

Shab-e-vasl thhi chaandni ka samaan thha
Baghal mein sanam thha khuda meherbaan thha
Mubaarak shab-e-qadr se bhi vo shab thhi
Seher tak mah o mushtari ka qiraan thha
Vo shab thhi ki thhi raushni jismein din ki
Zamiin par se ik noor ta aasmaan thha
Nikaale thhey do chaand uss ne muqaabil
Vo shab subah-e-jannat ka jis par gumaan thha

Aruusii ki shab ki halaavat thhi haasil
Farah-naak thhi rooh dil shaadmaan thha
Mushahid jamaal-e-pari ki thhi aankhein
Makaan-e-visal ik tilismi makaan thha
Huzoori nigahon ko deedaar se thhi
Khula thha vo parda ki jo darmiyaan thha
Kiya thha usse bosa-baazi ne paida
Kamar ki tarah se jo gha.eb dahaan thha
Haqeeqat dikhaata thha ishq-e-majaazi
Nihaan jis ko samjhe hue thhe ayaan thha
Bayaan khwaab ki tarah jo kar raha hai
Yeh kissa hai jabka ki Aatish javaan thha

The meeting was bathed in moonlight
Beside me the beloved, and merciful was the creator
More auspicious was the evening than the Night of Revelation
With Moon and Jupiter in embrace till dawn
What an evening it was sparkling like the light of day
Bright as paradise on earth
Two moons appeared one after the other
The night ending into heavenly morn
The sweetness of having become one
Spirits high and the heart happy
Witnessed by the wondrous eyes of beauty
In a magical abode
The look yearning to pay homage to appearance
The veil dropped from in between

Born of many kisses
Whose waist dissolved like the mouth
Imagined love turned to reality
What was puzzle became plain
This told like a dream by one
Is a story from when he was very young.

Nasikh

Zindagi zinda-dili ka hai naam
Murda-dil khaak jiya karte hain
Teri soorat se kisi ki nahin milti soorat
Hum jahaan mein teri tasveer liye phirte hain
Vo nahin bhoolta jahaan jaaun
Haaye main kya karun kahan jaaun

Liveliness is the name of living
Lifeless hearts do not live
None looks the way you do
I wander the world with your image
That I never forget
Alas! What do I do? Where do I go?

FIVE

Jurat, Rangin and Insha

Urdu poetry had begun to be enjoyed in the city in all its splendour as Lucknow was the new Mecca of the literati after Delhi and the Deccan. Local expressions had seeped into the idiom of Delhi, and the interpenetration of several languages emerged as Urdu as we know it today.

There was no binary between Urdu poetry written in Delhi and written later in Lucknow. Written in Lucknow, Urdu poetry is simply a continuation of earlier poetry, and poetry written in the same period in Delhi. The history of pre-modern Urdu literature is a delightful story not only about the rise and fall of language, but also of the shifting importance of cities strategically chosen and developed as centres of both literary and political power.

Among countless poets swarming the lanes of Lucknow in the early part of the nineteenth century, Shaikh Qalandar Baksh Jurat (d. 1809), Saadat Yaar Khan Rangin (d. 1835) and Insha Allah Khan (d. 1817) stood out as the soul of the city's cultural life. They were close friends and knew each other from Delhi.

Insha first came to Delhi when he was fifteen years old and no one could take their eyes away from his angelic face. The twinkle in his eyes had floored all those who met him, and his thick curly hair invited everyone to run their hand through it. In nineteenth-century Lucknow, the three of them were a favourite of the nobility. Audiences applauded each performance and recitation of the talented trio.

Jurat was a craze at court and was asked to repeat even cliches. His voice drowned in encores as he was requested to repeat the comparison he made of the beloved's beauty to the moon, her dark tresses to clouds pregnant with rain, and the look in her eyes to a fish darting swiftly in water.

Here Jurat confesses that her lips got locked with his once and he had licked his mouth for the rest of his life after that:

Mil gaye thhe ek baar usske jo mere lab se lab
Umr bhar honton pe apne main zabaan phera kiye

The writing of Jurat, Rangin and Insha was prolific and popular. All three wrote about playful love affairs, of desires that were possible to realise in this life, here and now. Jurat was the eldest of the three poets. His poetry is full of praise of pleasure and physical love. Unlike mystical poetry where the lover and beloved unite only in death, these poets celebrated the yearning and union of lovers in this life. It is the nature of mystical poetry to portray life as suffering and to keep lovers deprived of the company of each other. Bliss is possible only in death when it is impossible for the interfering world to prevent lovers from being with each other, like it was for Romeo and Juliet, Laila and Majnu, and Heer and Ranjha.

The earthly *aashiq*, the sufi lover, is united with the *mashooq*, or mystical beloved, only after death. In the sufi tradition, the most important event in life is death. All the sufi shrines celebrate *urs* and host festivities resembling a wedding on the death anniversary of a mystic. The Arabic word for wedding is urs and it is the annual urs that attracts most devotees in large numbers to the shrine of a favourite mystic. Mystics do not mourn death as the end of life but celebrate the occasion as the beginning of an existence that is at last in unity with the divine. Death is therefore an occasion to be celebrated like a wedding between the aashiq and his mashooq.

In contrast, Jurat describes the joy of physical love even between two women or two men, and between man and woman. There is also love between a man and a woman where the man is not the husband of the woman whose company he enjoys.

He says that the connection between beauty and love is natural. If the lover's longing did not exist, the beloved would have no meaning:

Hain laazim-o-malzoom baham husn-o-mohabbat
Hum hote na taalib jo vo matloob na hota

Jurat spent his childhood in Faizabad, moving to Lucknow in around 1800 to the court of Mirza Sulaiman Shikoh, the Mughal prince in self-exile. Jurat's poetry reflects the carefree atmosphere of Lucknow that was drenched in those days more in real romance and less in mystical consciousness. The population was madly in love with life, and with the ways of the material world. Jurat's writing reflects that life. It is hedonistic and worldly. He found the opportunity in Lucknow to explore different kinds of love in his writing, including that involving the same sex. The poet was born in Delhi and eventually lost his eyesight, but it is rumoured that early in life Jurat decided to fake blindness. The idea was to enjoy the company of women who revealed before him their true self. This way he was able to enjoy female beauty to his heart's content in every home and neighbourhood.

He raises his eyes towards her and the vision stares back as if wanting to know if he is not afraid of her:

Aankh uthaakar usse dekhoon hoon toh nazron mein mujhe
Yun jataata hai ki kya tujhko nahin darr mera

Jurat's poetry about sensuality, torrid love affairs and the joy of union between lovers in this life made him popular around the city.

Jurat sang endlessly in praise of beauty, same-sex love and amorous relations between women. He was an incurable lover by temperament and spent his life with those who enjoyed talking about poetry night and day. Many of his constant companions were courtesans. He was high-spirited, full of humour, welcomed by the elite and adored by people on the street as well. His audiences found him delightfully mischievous and quick-witted. In his poetry there is no pretence of grandeur and no vocabulary or thought too complicated for ordinary souls to grasp. He said what came to his heart but in such a way that the life of even the most unpoetic person began to crave romance. Jurat's physical appearance was not as flamboyant as Insha and Rangin, but he could overwhelm his audience even in modest attire. Despite being a darling of the nobility, his financial status remained precarious throughout his life.

When Jurat died in 1810, Nasikh wept that the poet of India was dead.

In the devil-may-care and hedonistic atmosphere of Lucknow, Jurat had found freedom to develop a new genre of poetry that talked of feminine desires. Rangin named this poetry *rekhti* as the female of rekhta. This poetry was based on women's feelings. The style became a craze at court. While rekhta has a male voice yearning for union with the creator, rekhti gives voice to the desire of the feminine for physical love with another woman, or a man. Here was an opportunity for men to explore their own emotions in rekhti and to verbalise their feelings even at the peril of sounding effeminate.

Rangin was a horse trader and soldier. He was known for his martial exploits. He knew a lot about horsemanship and wrote an entire book in verse on horses called the *Faras-nama-e Rangin* or *The Book of the Horse* that has been translated from Urdu into several languages.

But his love for bravery and his macho experience with horses did not prevent him from admitting that he was sick with longing for a courtesan. He had cried hard when he did not find his love. He was filled with anguish and left the neighbourhood she had lived in after writing a love lyric on the wall of her empty home.

Rangin wailed, where should he escape from love; love is everywhere he goes:

Ishq se bachke kidhar jayenge hum
Hai yeh maujood jidhar jayenge hum

Many experiments were done by writers during those carefree times. By the first quarter of the nineteenth century, Urdu poetry in Lucknow had shrugged off the trappings of decadent Persian poetry. The solace Urdu poetry brought to the life of the population was like a cool breeze in high summer. New elements were introduced to Urdu poetry, like satire, humour and erotica.

Early Persian poetry was influenced by Arabic models, including metre and rhyme like English poetry uses Latin metre and rhyme schemes. Up to the thirteenth century, most Persian poems, like their Arabic models, were in the form of an ode; the qasida that was written in praise of the creator of the world, or an earthly king. From the eleventh century, the lyrical love poem or ghazal was the dominant poetic form, celebrating love, both earthly and divine. To this day, Persian poetry remains the most extensive and refined expression of romantic emotion, steeped as it is in an all-inclusive world of beauty, compassion and love. The most lyrical of all love poetry is the ghazal that has earned a reputation of being the dignity, soul and heart of Urdu poetry.

Once poets writing in Persian in Lucknow had broken away from Arabic poetic forms like the rubai, the set of four rhymed lines was invented. The masnavi or epic poem is considered the greatest creation of classical Persian literature, especially in its ability to sustain poems of thousands of lines. Already in existence in the tenth century, the masnavi consists of three types of epics—the heroic from pre-Islamic Persian traditions, the romantic and the didactic.

The Urdu ghazal was popular with most poets. Its style is to bead together vocabulary into aching lyrics of love that pierce the heart of the listener like a dagger. The ghazal is traced back to Persian poetry where the emphasis is on love as a means to sense God by first loving everything in the world, including other human beings. The undying love expressed by the poet for an earthly beloved, a patron, or a sufi mentor is only a metaphor for the actual yearning for the ultimate beloved who is the creator of the world. At the same time, the total devotion and absolute obedience of the lover to the beloved becomes a symbol of complete surrender, devotion and obedience to the same power. *Layla wa-Majnun* has mystical overtones that characterise most Persian love poetry, especially because the love described between the lovers Layla and Majnun is full of unconditional devotion and obedience to the beloved without expectation of reward.

In contrast to mystical love, which is the main theme of rekhta or classical Urdu poetry, Insha and Rangin developed rekhti to focus on a female speaker who is not interested in marriage or in a long-term commitment with a lover. The sole interest of the voice in rekhti is a desire for pleasure. There is no celebration of husband, children, family, marriage, or God in rekhti, but only of the amorous desire of human beings.

Rangin wants to know how long he should remain separated from the beloved; how long he should remain devoid of love:

Judaa uss se bhala kab tak rahoon main
Bari uss se bhala kab tak rahoon main

In rekhti, the female voice talks mostly of the intensity experienced when human beings are attracted to each other physically. Poets also include in their writing other activities of everyday life of women like grooming, singing, cooking and sewing. The use of everyday language and the description of women's amorous relationship with each other is a distinctive feature of rekhti. This innovative style of writing is representative of the cosmopolitan character of Urdu poetry written in Lucknow at a time when the city had blossomed into a centre of a flourishing Indo-Persian culture. A culture that was also inspired by age-old local traditions like the Kamasutra and the romance between Lord Krishna and the married Radha of Vrindavan. However, the needs of human beings for pleasure were soiled in the post-colonial period. Pleasure as an emotion was undermined by imported Victorian values and denounced as obscene. The history of same-sex love in South Asia has ever since followed colonial ideas of morality, mistaking them for a tradition of their own. Over time, the conquered population even internalised and imitated the puritan ways of the conquerors. In pre-colonial times, Lucknow was described as an obscene place where lust was worship. Here obscene verses and longing for same-sex love was common and unique not just to rekhti or rekhta but characteristic of all *Lakhnavi* (belonging to the city of Lucknow in north India) poetry.

Unlike Rangin, who was almost forgotten because he wrote vulgar verses, Insha found respectability not because he was a rekhti poet but because he wrote a book on Urdu grammar. He is best remembered for the story of Rani Ketki where Insha does not use any Arabic or Persian vocabulary. But many Urdu critics frown at Insha's naughty ghazals in colloquial language full of erotic imagery. Post-colonial Urdu critics dismiss most of the writing of rekhti poets as crude and immoral. Much of it is lost and it is Rangin's reputation that has suffered most as he is associated solely with rekhti writing and for attracting attention to himself for the outlandish manner in which he used to dress. Rangin covered his head with scarfs in resplendent colours.

All those who see 'rangin' as bad, can he remain good with them for long?

Bura mujhko samajhta hai jo 'rangin'
Bhali uss se bhala kab tak rahoon main

Rangin was born Saadat Yaar Khan in Sirhind in Punjab. He was brought up in Delhi and was employed as a soldier. For a while he had traded in horses. Rangin's personality was as colourful as his name and whatever he wrote was enjoyed by his fans—from romantic rekhti verses to the *farasnama*, his story about horses.

Rangin's close association with the beauties of Lucknow instilled in him an understanding of feminine feelings that are ignored in societies around the world. Rangin developed rekhti as the voice of the feminine gender, introducing a very interesting trait in literature. In the rekhti style, the poet talks of love, life and longing from a woman's point of view. Rangin's rekhti is playful, cheerful and celebratory of sex rather than judgemental or satirical.

However, critics fail to understand why the non-mystical rekhti poetry that was inspired by the romance of everyday life became so popular with the pleasure-loving population of the time. Why did everyone crave the company of the fairy-faced Insha, from the king to the beauties of the bazaar? One minute, Insha was seen kissing the royal hand at court and the very next he was in the home of female friends helping them to choose the apt perfume and an outfit to match for a night out at a mushaira.

Insha's patron was Saadat Ali Khan, the sixth ruler of Avadh till 1814. The ruler was in love with a courtesan who loved another man. Saadat did not punish the courtesan for not responding to His Majesty's desire. He was most considerate towards the feeling of the one he loved. He requested the courtesan to keep him company for a few hours each day and later return to her lover. This royal highness saw no joy in forcing a human being to love him when her heart was distracted. The ruler found contentment in helping the object of his love find peace and happiness.

Insha put into his poetry what he found in the lap of his favourite women. He spent a lot of time cuddling and caressing women, whispering verses from behind French chiffon dupattas soaked in scents like sandalwood. He sang eulogies here and recited obituaries there and dazzled the city with his wit. Insha had peppered his writing with many English words as he went around town on an elephant. He even wrote about the romance between his elephant Bahadur and Chanchal Pyari.

A majority of the people identified more with the lovers of rekhti. In rekhti literature, the beloved is not a symbol of an unseen god, but a human being with whom the poet enjoys a happy relationship without guilt. Non-mystical poetry talks of pleasure here and now in this world. The rekhti poetry of Jurat, Insha and Rangin is not a stepping stone for the male lover's yearning for union with the beloved, who is a male god, in death. The theme in non-mystical rekhta poetry and in rekhti challenges classical poetry's ideal of perfect love as framed by separation and suffering in this world.

Writes Professor Ruth Vanita in *Gender, Sex and the City, Urdu Rekhti Poetry 1780–1870*: 'the hallmark of rekhti and non-mystical rekhta writing is an awareness of hybridity, not just of language and culture, but also of people.'

For Vanita, rekhti is serious business. Following Johan Huizinga's ground-breaking approach to culture and especially poetry as play, Vanita says that rekhti's poetic playfulness is not non-serious; it is a manifestation of a worldview capable of profound depth but also of lightness, happiness as well as reflection, piety as well as profanity.

The word rekhta literally means mixing or pouring different things into a mould to create a new compound, and Urdu poetry began as macaronic verse which mixed local words with Persian.

The poetic persona of Insha is naughty, teasing and full of laughter and mirth. Insha praises his own poetry as playful, and eroticism is only one part of his play with words. His sympathies are with women who enjoy life instead of those who choose to suffer and see themselves as a victim. For Insha, pleasure is as genuine as pain. Insha's rekhti explores the feelings of women whose life does not revolve around relationships with men; instead, it brings into focus relationships that women have with each other. Men are placed by rekhti poets to the periphery, bringing the world of women centre stage to the poetic universe.

Opinion makers of the time felt that acceptance of the coexistence of male and female presence in life helps to avoid the uncalled-for valorisation or condemnation of people based on biological sex or gender. And recognition of the existence of a female within every man and the masculine in every woman focuses on the centrality of the human being, be it male or female, thus blurring the binaries of sex and gender celebrated by society.

The respect for the female voice can still be found in mythology. And it is cultural memory that has saved society from becoming hopelessly puritan. What has watered down liberality considerably is the idea that Victorian puritanism introduced by the British colonialists in India is an integral part of *sanatan dharm* and *Bharatiya sanskriti*.

According to Professor Purushottam Agrawal, author of *Kabir Kabir*, Indic religious traditions in early modern India were enriched by its encounter with Islam:

> In the Islamic context, poets, sufi or not, had long challenged the authoritarian censorious and vindictive nature of religious and political power structures. Only in such an enriched context in which poets resisted authority could a poet like Jayasi have celebrated love and beauty in so uninhibited a manner without causing outrage. In fact, the poet was greatly admired and respected. Apart from Kabir, many poets across the country adopted the voices of women without provoking widespread anger.

Surely rekhti poets were influenced by medieval erotic poetry and romance narratives written also in Braj Bhasha, the local language spoken in large parts of the region. The refreshing aspect of rekhti is that it makes love earthy and enjoyable, unlike mystic poetry that leads lovers on a journey towards death before they are united, displaying a disturbing affection for death over life.

Vanita describes non-mystical rekhta as mainstream Urdu poetry with a male speaker focusing on everyday life in this world. Mir Taqi Mir's beloved in the eighteenth century is already female, but with mystical dimensions. The spirit of rekhti is not mystical; it is physical and material. Female relationships with each other are the hallmark of Lucknow rekhti. The speech of rekhti is colloquial and the speaker is female conversing with a male over explicit sexual interactions like in common rekhta verses.

Insha and Rangin's rekhti is distinct in being heavily female-oriented, where both the lover and beloved are women. The themes of rekhti throb with the urgency of living their one and only life in pleasure. Insha's verses provide added pleasure because parts of his poetry are also hilarious.

Rangin met Insha for the last time under tragic circumstances. Rangin had not seen Insha for nearly a decade. When he returned to Lucknow, the first thing he did was to look up Insha. Insha had moved from Sulaiman Shikoh's palace to the royal court. He was thrilled at first but then felt exhausted in the role of entertainer rather than poet. He was tired of producing verses on command and at forcing himself to laugh at royalty's juvenile jokes.

Rangin was devastated to see Insha. Insha cried when he saw Rangin and crying, he led his friend into his home. Rangin noticed that the front door was hanging on its hinges. Elephants had once guarded the same door to Insha's home.

Insha's wife who answered Rangin's knock on the door was dressed worse than a servant. Inside, the home was littered with dusty pots and pans, some of them broken. Insha made

Rangin sit on the floor on a straw mat and trembled while looking at Rangin.

'I fanned him and offered him iced water, watermelon and mangoes. This was Insha? If you remember, Insha was once the life of feasts and festivals. Insha—who had brought out humour in everyday life. Now there were no more poems, no more jokes. We sat together and wept—the only thing left for us to do now,' recalled Rangin, who had kept an open house throughout his life and hosted mushairas that were the favourite avenues of get-togethers of a great many beauties of the land.

Soon after the meeting with his friend, Insha passed away in 1817, while a heartbroken Rangin continued to live till 1835.

Women had attended poetic gatherings hosted by Insha and Rangin in large numbers. Perhaps women from traditional families did not, but courtesans had looked forward to meetings with the well-known poets of the day. Courtesans had also hosted mushairas where they recited verses written by them, and Insha and Rangin were always present in their midst. They sang together and danced to love lyrics.

Women were well versed in Urdu and Persian and had engaged educated men in discussions over matters of this world and the world beyond. The status between a courtesan and respectable women had been bridged. Many members of the nobility married courtesans and spent long hours with women who were not nobility, but were talented. The lives of these women were not secluded but lively; there was nothing gloomy and isolated about their existence. Many patrons and poets made women's lives inclusive by using vocabulary they had brought to the city from dialects spoken by them in the countryside. Many words picked up by poets while in the company of women were included in their writing. The easy conversation between women, and sometimes between women and men, provided excellent content to rekhti poems. But rekhti is not exclusively about same-sex relationships. It is also about everyday conversations among courtesans in playful and naughty idioms.

The worldly, hedonistic and happy love life of two married women and their amorous relationship with each other is captured in many writings that are sprinkled liberally with colloquial vocabulary used mostly by women.

Jurat wrote *Chaptinama*, in the erotic subgenre style where female speakers openly declare their preference for women over men, and together with like-minded women, they enjoy the sharing and exchange of betel leaves, flowers and perfume. The act of sexual play between women is *chapti* and Ruth Vanita calls it play without a dildo. Says Jurat on behalf of a female that compared to pleasure with her female lover where is the pleasure in men?

Aisi lazzat kahaan hai mardon mein
Jaisi lazzat du-gana chapti mein

While the attraction of men for other men is well known, the unique feature of pre-colonial Lakhnavi poetry is the depiction of relationships of women with women. The importance of this poetry is its depiction of cross-sex romance and same-sex romance as nonchalantly as conventional romance. The writers respect relationships between two women like they do between man and a woman, to say that the emotional response of all lovers is similar irrespective of their gender. It was acceptance of the fact that one woman can love many times and many men, without her reputation being soiled as an inferior human being.

From the margins of urban existence, rekhti had lifted women to the centre, projecting them as important influencers of urban culture, especially urban speech. Patronage also helped women to upgrade their lot in society. The first wife of the rulers of the region was invariably a princess. But those in power would tie the knot with many courtesans and servants, showering titles and wealth upon them. Such acts of love by those in power improved the social status of women, most of whom often came from depressed social and economic families from the suburbs of Lucknow. In Delhi there is the example of Udham Bai, a courtesan who became Mughal Emperor Muhammad Shah's third wife. Her son Ahmad Shah Bahadur was the next emperor and she managed the empire for six years. There was Lal Kanwar who was the life of Delhi, Agra and Lahore once. Lal Kanwar was witty and flirtatious. She stole the heart of Mughal Emperor Jahandar Shah with her superb singing style and dance performances. After Jahandar Shah saw her dance for the first time, he had swept Lal Kanwar off the floor and carried her in his arms to a room where she sang for him till the lark announced a new dawn. Lal Kanwar had lived at the Red Fort and was given the title of Imtiaz Mahal—her memorial still stands on the premises of Delhi's Golf Club. After she became queen, Lal Kanwar brought Zohra, a friend, fellow dancer and vegetable vendor, to court to bestow upon her respect due to noblewomen.

The ghazal, the love lyrics, was the pride of Urdu poetry and had traditionally been a male domain. Both the narrator, as the lover, and the beloved had a male voice, providing patriarchal conventions ample space to explore the genre, including eroticism. Like their exclusion from the public sphere, the door for women in pre-modern ghazal was also shut. Then came rekhti written in an exaggerated feminine voice by a male poet to highlight women's issues. Rekhti coined new names like *dugana*, *yagana*, *zanakhi*, *begana*, *shakhi*, *ilachi*, *wari* and *pyari* for the female beloved, by a gender-friendly poet like Rangin. However, in the long run, men speaking in the female voice could not substitute for the absence of women in life. The theme of rekhti is not homosexuality alone but the day-to-day conversation among courtesans in playful and witty idioms that are also captured in rekhti writing. Rangin's poetry may focus more on a sexual theme where the poet wonders why the dugana has tied a dildo to herself as it only hurts her lover who worries for her womb.

Insha celebrates lesbian love by groaning that the neighbour came to take fire and she lit up desire in the heart.

Lene aag lene ko jo aayin toh kahin laag laga
Bibi hamsaai ne di jee mein meri aag laga

Some rekhti is most playful. Jan Sahab who died in 1886 wrote that the idiot took his tongue in his mouth a thousand times and became a Muslim, he is no kaafir:

Le chuka munh me hai lallu meri
Sau bar zubaan ho gaya kab ka musalmaan
Yeh kya kaafir hai

One style of rekhti is *saraapa* or from head to toe wherein the poet takes delight in describing different parts of the lover's body. Says Jurat about the feet of the beloved that to take them in the hand is strangely pleasurable, and then he would like to make her sit and watch him enjoy.

Aur jo haathon mein utha lu'n toh ajab lutf uthaaun
Phir jo vo lutf uthaana tujhe bithaake dikhlaaun

In rekhti love knows no bounds.

Purists see rekhti as puerile. The language used in rekhti is dismissed as the everyday conversation of women heard routinely in most households. Rangin who assembled this language into rekhti writing is waved aside as not worth remembering. Rangin's friendship with women and the time he spent in the company of courtesans and dancing girls is not appreciated by some critics. Jan Sahab, who also wrote rekhti and recited his work in public dressed like a woman, is dismissed as a buffoon.

In Lucknow, Ghazi-ud-Din Haider, the son and successor of Saadat Ali, was a lover of beauty, and courtiers would introduce their daughters to him in the hope that he would marry them. Wajid Ali Shah, the last king, improved the lot of more than 300 humble women by performing temporary marriages with them in a tradition called *muta*, meaning pleasure, and common amongst Shia Muslims.

Lucknow played a remarkable role in providing refuge to the literati, and to Urdu literary activities, as the Mughal capital of Delhi was laid to waste. By allowing talent to unleash creativity, the city helped to safeguard important aspects of the shared heritage and culture of the region.

The rekhti style of poetry was crucial in focusing attention on female feelings—feelings which society pretends do not exist. The recognition of the pivotal role of the female population in society trickled into prose writing as well. Syed Agha Husain Amanat Lakhnavi included numerous female dancers in *Indra Sabha*, a popular opera-like drama he wrote in 1852.

The story unfolds in the heavenly palace of Indra, king of gods, who is surrounded by the glitter of gold and silver fairies in different colours of the rainbow. Sabz Pari, an emerald green fairy from his entourage, falls in love with Gulfam, an earthly prince. The lovelorn fairy uses black magic to smuggle Gulfam into the celestial world of Indra who is so annoyed at the intrusion that he clips the wings of the fairy and drops Gulfam into the well of darkness. The fairy is fearless in her love for Gulfam—representing the passion of the heavens for earth. She does everything that is in her power to free her lover. The fairy's mesmerising dance and singing melt Indra's heart, earning Gulfam's release. Indra blesses the couple to be together forever.

Indra Sabha written in verse is not just entertainment but symbolic of the breathless attraction between all opposite forces like heaven and earth, man and woman, Hindu and Muslim, and rural and urban. The same theme inspires high culture as well as folk culture from the ghazal, thumri, holi, *chaubola* to the chhand.

Indra Sabha unites not only Gulfam and the Sabz Pari, but also a Vedic deity like Indra to a story of Islamic origin, making it the pride of the newly emerging Indo-Muslim theatre.

The reputation of *Indra Sabha* spread to Europe and it was translated into German by Friedrich Rosen in 1892, dominating the theatrical world till the arrival of the talky cinema in the twentieth century. This way the *Indra Sabha* accelerated a process that shared court-based styles of music, dance and poetry with the population at large.

In his narrative poem *Khwaja Hasan and Courtesan Bakhshi*, a romance with a courtesan heroine, Jurat steers away from ideas of conventional love. The unconventional element in his narrative is that the beloved is a courtesan and the poem elaborates on the relationship between her and her Sufi mystic lover that ends not in marriage but in acceptance by society. The mystic goes back and forth from the courtesan's home because he cannot live without her. In an earlier line, the mystic says that he is unable to describe his beloved's courage who is a beautiful woman but has a man's virtues. Their mutual love continues to bloom on earth with the blessings of the almighty.

Courtesans were addressed lovingly as *pari* or fairies. The abode of courtesans who were part of the *Indra Sabha* performances was not a kotha or brothel but called the *parikhana* and located inside the Qaiserbagh palace of Wajid Ali Shah, the last ruler of Lucknow. Inside the Qaiserbagh palace complex was built a *rahaskhana*, a special room for enacting the amorous exploits of Lord Krishna and his female devotees. Wajid Ali Shah hosted open-air performances of the *Indra Sabha* in the gardens of Qaiserbagh and he often played the role of Raja Indra. He liked to be surrounded by countless fairies dressed in different colours. Wajid Ali Shah also played Lord Krishna, and the same female dancers performing the role of fairies in *Indra Sabha* were transformed into lovelorn milkmaids longing for the company of Lord Krishna. Wajid Ali Shah wrote a play called *The Story of Radha and Krishna* that was performed in Qaiserbagh in 1843. The costume, scenery, language, music and narration style of *Indra Sabha* were widely emulated also out of nostalgia for the monarchy that ended three years after the play was staged. From post-colonial times, the aristocratic feel of *Indra Sabha* seeped down to the lanes of Lucknow, blurring the divide between the ways of the court and life on the street. The kathak dances, the songs of the thumri, ghazal and doha combined with basant, holi, dadra, saavan and bihag styles of singing into a musical diversity that went hand in hand with a new style in stagecraft that added a pinch of chutzpah into the folk performances as well.

The *Indra Sabha* is not only Urdu's but also north India's first full-length play in modern times and it played a very important role in reviving the great tradition of Sanskrit plays. Performances of *Indra Sabha* were witnessed in village after village and its popularity spread beyond South Asia when it was translated into German in 1892.

Wajid Ali Shah had an eye for talented people like Amanat. To stage the stories of Radha and Krishna, and of Raja Indra, he had required lots of female dancers in times when respectable women did not publicly dance or sing.

In *Awadh under the Nawabs*, author Surendra Mohan writes:

> Wajid Ali Shah had provided a modern stage to Lucknow. He needed female actresses. Since the stage was not considered to be a fitting place where respectable citizenry should make its appearance, Wajid Ali Shah contracted many muta marriages, and those ladies acted on the stage of Lucknow.

Marriage to the ruler also made the actresses and dancers loyal to him. Two nawabs before him were poisoned with the help of the British, and Wajid Ali Shah perceived a constant threat to his life. Some of the women were trained soldiers, and because he had married them, they guarded his life with supreme loyalty, leaving him free to read and to write. Wajid Ali Shah was a poet and prolific writer. He wrote nearly fifty books of poems, drama, history religion, music, dance and a royal book of rules and regulations called *dastoor-e-wajidi*, a comprehensive documentation of government actions and policies for public welfare. He left the world with a library full of love lyrics, letters and diaries all of which wait to be read, interpreted, translated by many more, and to be shared with a larger audience. During his rule till 1856, Wajid Ali Shah had employed 1700 poets in his court, and he was fond of experimenting with different styles of poetry writing from the romantic ghazal to the masnavi and the marsiya. The verses he composed were both sensual as well as spiritual.

His collection of songs in *Geet Najo* and *Dulhan* are based on different forms of singing like dhrupad, sargam, hori, khayal, tarana, tappa, thumri, dadra and folk.

He wrote that the poet keeps no shield or sword because he is free-spirited, and his swagger is that of a wanderer.

Dhaal rakhta nahin talwaar nahin
Shayar hoon chaal bhi meri faqirana hai
Aazaad hoon main

Wajid Ali Shah chose Akhtar (star) as his pen name. He wrote, 'In Lucknow these days, oh Akhtar, your oratory is full of praise':

Aaj kal Lucknow mein ae Akhtar
Dhoom hai teri khush-bayani ki

Jurat

Ab ishq tamasha mujhe dikhlaaye hai kuchh aur
Kehta hoon kuchh aur munh se nikal jaaye hai kuchh aur
Naaseh ki himaaqat toh zara dekhiyo yaaron
Samjha hoon main kuchh aur mujhe samjhaaye hai kuchh aur
Kya deeda-e-Ihoon-baar se nisbat hai ki yeh abr
Barsaaye hai kuchh aur voh barsaaye kuchh aur
Rone de ha'nsaa mujhko na hamdam ki tujhe ab
Kuchh aur hii bhaata hai mujhe bhaaye hai kuchh aur
Paighambar aaya hai yeh ausaan ga'nvaaye
Poochhoon hoon main kuchh aur mujhe batlaaye hai kuchh aur
'Jurat' ki tarah mere havaas ab nahin bar ja
Kehta hoon kuchh aur munh se nikal jaaye hai kuchh aur

Love is now a different tale
I want to say something, but something else is what I wail
What ill advice from a friend
I know something and he wants me to something else pretend
Is this related to tears or is a drink?
Something rains but it rains something else he thinks

Let me cry, do not make me laugh now
I need something and something else for you is wow
The message to me is to forget
I ask for something and something else is what I get
I desire no longer like 'Jurat', go away
I want to say something but something else is what I say.

Rangin

Ishq se bach ke kidhar jayenge hum
Hai yeh maujood jidhar jayenge hum
Tan ke bas rakhiye qabza par haath
Dekhiye muft mein dar jayenge hum
Teri dehleez par apne sar ko
Ek din kaatke dhar jayenge hum
Vo yeh kehte hain na de dil hum ko
Dekh lete hi mukar jayenge hum
Manaa karte ho ab bas yaaro aaj
Usske ghar jaayenge par jayenge hum
Dil ki leni hai khabar humko zaroor
Aaj toh phir bhi udhar jayenge hum
Dum kahin lenge na phir ta-ba-adam
Tere kooche se agar jayenge hum
Tu na guzrega jafaa se zaalim
Jaan se apni guzar jayenge hum
Zeest baaki hai toh apna 'Rangin'
Naam iss ishq mein kar jayenge hum

Where can I hide from love? It is wherever I go
Carefully caress the body without frightening me so
On your doorstep my head one day I will lay
Don't give me your heart, they say
I will refuse, and that will be the day
You refuse, 'That is enough for the day,' you say
I will go to his house, I will, to find out if the
heart beats still
I will not rest if your home I don't see
You may not know such pain
My life, however, will end in vain
But if life remains then your 'Rangin'
Will make eternal his love for you, his queen.

Insha

Neend maston ko kahaan aur kidhar ka takiya
Khisht-e-khum-khana hai yaan apne toh sar ka takiya
Lakht-e-dil aa ke musafir se theherte hain yahaan
Chashm hai humse gadaaon ki guzar ka takiya
Jis taraf aankh utha dekhiye ho jaaye asar
Hum toh rakhte hain faqat apni nazar ka takiya
Chain hargiz nahin makhmal ke usse takiye par
Uss pari ke liye ho hoor ke par ka takiya

No question of sleep for the intoxicated,
No question of a pillow
A brick of the tavern cushions the head
Those that the heart loves pause here

Have nots have the comfort of a pillow from the likes of us
Wherever the look rests there is an effect
The only pillow that I carry is of my vision
There is no comfort on a pillow of velvet
For that fairy only a pillow made from the wings of angels will do.

SIX

The Land of Fairies

All through the nineteenth century, Lucknow resembled a ghazal most gorgeous. It had blossomed into a city more beautiful than Babylon, with its bustling bazaars and amazing architecture, not to forget its golden cupolas and silver minarets shimmering like molten gold amidst sylvan surroundings. Visitors rubbed their eyes and marvelled at the fairyland they stood in.

Writes Abdul Halim Sharar, nineteenth-century essayist, historian and novelist:

> In those days the population and splendour of Lucknow increased to such an extent that it would not be out of place to call it the Babylon of India.

Apart from *kunds*, imambaras, mosques, temples, gardens and water tanks, people visited libraries opened in every neighbourhood. The populations had enjoyed an observatory, lithography and a printing press in Lucknow that was home to Sanskrit, Persian and Arabic scholars and European astronomers, barbers, gardeners and librarians. It was a seat of learning as well as a playground for pageants. Festivals were celebrated all year round by communities belonging to different castes and creeds. Hospitality was at its best. Most citizens had kept an open house and visited each other's homes dressed in attires stylishly cut out of fine muslin cloth often embroidered in white thread and dabbed in musk, ambergris and other fragrant oils extracted from flowers and herbs. An array of delicacies had remained permanently spread out on the *dastarkhwan* of even humble homes, and many hookah-puffing begums had played host to painters, engineers and poets. In imitation of the many poets in the city, vendors had hawked their ware to the rhythm of horses constantly galloping to and fro on busy streets, and in vocabulary borrowed from different languages of *khadi boli*, Urdu, Persian, English, even French.

The seller of precious stones had beckoned with, 'Sir, tell your jeweller how he can serve you':

Miyaan saheb jawahir ko bataaiye kaam

The flower-seller promised jasmine blossoms soaked in fragrance:

Muattar phool hain ji motiyake

The sugarcane juice vendor swearing that the juice was sweeter than sugar:

Misri ke ganne

Hawking lip-smacking spicy chickpea snacks—hot, crisp, salted with chillies and lemon juice:

Kya namkeen bane hain
Mirchon ke chane hain ... karare bhur bhure nimbu ke ras ke hain

Marvellous buildings were hidden behind majestic trees standing along crowded streets. The threshold of houses lined endlessly on both sides of the riverbank had glowed with a different hue at every twilight, at dawn and before dark. The Gomti river was flush with hectic trade, and after dark, once the full moon was sighted, pleasure activities were hosted on the waterway, especially for poets. Drowned in so much poetry, the city began to imagine itself as the most bewitching poem of the time.

As if in anticipation of the ghazal that Lucknow was gradually becoming, Mir Taqi Mir, greatest of all ghazal composers, had rhapsodised a few decades earlier:

Shafaq se hain dar-o-diwaar zard shaam-o-seher
Hua hai Lakhnau iss rahguzar mein pilibhit

Mir tries to capture the daily vision of violet upon azure that he witnessed every sunrise, and at sunset when the thresholds of the city were bathed in yellow, orange and red of the sun. The shimmering rays of the setting sun had drenched even the mud walls of humble homes into molten gold.

Fanny Parkes, an Englishwoman, had lived in India till 1845. She was invited to Lucknow's Badshah Bagh, once a pleasure garden with three palaces and a *hammam*, or steam bath. At the centre of Badshah Bagh was an open hall supported by finely carved pillars where festive gatherings were held. Between the pleasant walks, gaily hued flowers had bordered shallow marble lakes filled with sweet-scented rose water at the Badshah Bagh. A tiger in a cage was an added attraction there.

In *Wanderings of a Pilgrim in Search of the Picturesque* published by her in 1850, Parks talks about the Badshah Bagh where the Lucknow University stands today.

> There is a hammam containing rooms heated to different temperatures, the heat of each increasing until you arrive at the steam bath itself. On the left of the garden is the third palace sacred to the ladies of the *zenana*. This house is built of marble and covered with flower work of pounded talc which has exactly the appearance of silver, giving an eastern style to the place. There are two handsome gateways, a steam engine to supply the fountains and a superb tiger in a cage.

Economic historians claim that north India in the early nineteenth century had a stable banking system and flourishing trade in cotton, indigo, metals, grains and luxury goods. From 1775 onwards, Lucknow, Avadh's capital, emerged as the richest and perhaps most culturally significant centre of its day. When Wajid Ali Shah, the last ruler of Lucknow, ascended the throne in 1847, the love lyric had ruled over the hearts and minds of poetry lovers. The amorous desires expressed by the new gods of poetry like Rind Lakhnavi, Wazir Ali Saba Lakhnavi and Mirza Shauq Lakhnavi were much more in demand.

Shauq was a physician who wrote ghazals. His mentor was Aatish. Shauq was as fun-loving as the atmosphere of Lucknow of that time. Mischievously he points to himself as enough proof of divine mercy, as he continues to sin in every possible way.

Sabit yeh kar raha hoon ki rehmat-shanaas hoon
Har qism ka gunaah kiye ja raha hoon main

Wajid Ali Shah himself wrote achingly romantic verses, describing the beloved as one with a deceptive waistline. Her mouth is a knot, eyes that of a gazelle—the fairy-faced, whose abdomen like a fish, figure so fragrant, the forehead like a river, speech as sweet as of Jesus.

Kamar dhoka dahan uqda gazaal ankhein pari chehra
Shikam heera badan khushboo jabin dariya zabaan iisa

Sauda's satires and Mir's ghazals exploring spirituality were less popular. Mir was almost forgotten despite his sensual writings like in this couplet where the poet finds the body of the beloved beautiful when it is revealed through her sweat-soaked blouse like the rose whose beauty is veiled within layers upon layers of petals:

Goondh ke goya patti gul ki voh tarkeeb banai hai
Ran badan ka tab dekho jab choli bheege paseene mein

Poetry lovers preferred the compositions of Nasikh and the verses of Aatish. Wajid Ali Shah chose Aatish as his mentor. While the basic structure of Urdu poetry remained the same, there was a change in theme and in the use of language. Both poets and the people were more attracted to the physical world than the philosophical. Over decades, the Urdu poet began by serenading an earthly beloved. The poet addressed her by name and endlessly praised her physical beauty and irresistible mannerisms. The poet admitted to secret meetings with her, complaining why he could not stay with her longer, in fact forever. At some stage, the real beloved lost her identity to an abstract idea of love whose gender was not clear. The poet could be crooning to a same-sex love, or swooning over someone from the opposite sex. It was difficult to say. Some poets were inspired to elevate the stature of the beloved to a more spiritual idea at par with the creator of the world who was imagined as absolute beauty and as ultimate love.

During the reign of Wajid Ali Shah, the many cultural activities had overpowered the senses. The poetry was sensual and meant to provide pleasure. The poets enjoyed the freedom to eulogise a woman's physical beauty and to pen details of the attractive clothes and jewellery worn by women. The melancholic mood that had dominated themes in Urdu poetry written earlier was replaced with literature and public performances that made citizens happy. Most in demand were heartfelt love stories. The Radha and Krishna stories were popular. Many a narrative detailing an author's adventures with beauties of the bazaar had thrilled audiences. The lifestyle in Wajid Ali Shah's Lucknow was voluptuous. He built Qaiserbagh south of present-day Hazratganj. The palace complex of Qaiserbagh was dotted with buildings with brass domes painted in saffron. The balustrades where in shining white while the windows in green were often decorated with orange curtains. Apart from sprawling living quarters, government offices, gateways and bazaars, there was a large rectangular courtyard flanked on each side by terraces of two-storeyed houses with smaller courtyards. The Lanka building stood centre stage like an open-air theatre of rooftop height with a stream flowing below the raised platform. The Lanka was flanked by free-standing pavilions that were lit from the inside, and where performances were held for guests personally invited by Wajid Ali Shah.

Wajid Ali Shah was in love with the *rahas* performances that celebrated Lord Krishna's amorous dalliance with countless milkmaids of Vrindavan. He had collected a huge ensemble of pretty, young women with a talent for dance and music, but most of them were from economically depressed families from the countryside. Since neither poverty nor musical performances were considered respectable, Wajid Ali Shah married the young women to provide them respect and acceptability amongst the city's nobility. The female artistes resided within the Qaiserbagh palace complex in a place especially built for them called the *parikhana.* The artistes were addressed as fairies who performed in the dance dramas staged within the palace complex. The dancers were divided into different groups of red and green fairies and they also played the role of gopis, the milkmaids in love with Lord Krishna when he had lived with his foster parents in the verdant forest area of Vrindavan, in Mathura district, about 400 km west of Lucknow, tending to cattle and playing the flute all day long.

Wajid Ali Shah loved to play the part of Krishna in the performances he staged at Qaiserbagh. Once a year Wajid Ali Shah hosted a fair when the gates of Qaiserbagh were opened to the public that was allowed to participate in the opulent lifestyle of royalty. Wajid Ali Shah had dressed like a yogi in a saffron robe. His curled hair was spread across the shoulder and his forehead was smeared with ash made from pearls burnt and crushed into powder. In this garb, the ruler of Avadh had met ordinary citizens who had visited him also wearing ochre-coloured clothes in the palace to pay respect to the yogi-king, and to participate in the frolicking hosted for the entire city by Wajid Ali Shah. On that festive occasion, the city had resembled an ocean of saffron.

The appreciation of Hindi poetry only enriched the composite culture of Avadh. Writes Surendra Mohan in his book, *Awadh under the Nawabs*:

> The area of Bilgram in Hardoi district of Avadh produced several Muslim poets who wrote in Hindi. They adopted Hindi expressions and gave a new meaning to Islamic ideas. They also adopted some elements of Hindu philosophy and the legend of Krishna to give a more meaningful concept to society at large ... this was a time of great creativity in Hindi literature. The period is known as *riti kaal* when poetry of love and *sringar* (idyllic romance) was the idiom of the day.

To celebrate Basant at springtime, citizens would step out into the city dressed in yellow clothes, inspiring poets to sing some more.

'Friend, are you aware today that Spring is here, the splendour of spring is obvious everywhere,' says Ufuq Lakhnavi:

> *Saaqi kuchh aaj tujhko khabar hai basant ki*
> *Har su bahaar pesh-e-nazar hai basant ki*

Whether it was Basant, Eid, Holi, or Navroz, the Parsi new year, the whole city participated in celebrations sponsored by the rulers. The name *Ufuq* means horizon in Arabic and it was adopted by Munshi Dwarka Prasad as his pen name. Ufuq was born in Lucknow in 1864. He was fluent in Sanskrit, Hindi, Persian, Urdu and English and was loved for his sense of humour. Ufuq began to compose poetry when he was nine years old and it did not take him long to become famous. Towards the end of the nineteenth century, patriotism had crept into Urdu poetry as an inspiring theme for poets. Addressing Indians both Hindu and Muslim, Ufuq calls upon them to together make the country the envy of paradise. Irrigate the wondrous garden with the blood of your love, wrote Ufuq.

Rashk-e-jinaan banao Hindustan ko mil kar
khoon-e-jigar se seencho iss gulistan ko mil kar

Muharram is the first month of the Islamic calendar. This is the time of the year when merrymaking would be halted and the city would go into a state of mourning. For almost sixty-eight days, the landscape of the city would be dyed in black as citizens wore clothes in the ritual colour of grief. Gaiety was exchanged for grief, and beginning with the first day of Muharram, Lucknow was converted into Karbala, the desert city on the banks of the river Euphrates in modern-day Iraq.

Lucknow took a break from fun and frolic during Muharram. All colourful clothing was folded away at this time of the year. In solidarity with the belief of Shia Muslims, citizens would dress in black. Despite the sombre mood, some residents remembered to keep their black attire stylish and many found the disarray in which the hair of the women in mourning fell on the face seductive.

The *tawaif* looked attractive even in her state of simplicity during the month of mourning. Tawaifs played a significant role in the religious and cultural reorientation of Lucknow in the nineteenth century and were the sole custodian of a complex high culture and traditions. Their artistic soul was a rich reservoir of refined living. They were trendsetters and their lifestyle was seen as the epitome of sophisticated existence. They observed the rituals of Muharram to the letter. They performed each formality with the same passion that they put into entertaining their audience with song and dance during the rest of the year. The tawaif community were ardent devotees of Husain. Most of them were well versed in classical music and attracted large audiences that came to listen to them recite the *nauha* at a majlis. Those who could afford to had built an imambara. Others would convert a corner of their home into a temporary imambara where they hosted majlis before a tableau of the *tazia*. The word tazia is from consolation colours of the tombs of Hasan and Husain that are taken in a procession to a local place called Karbala for burial on the tenth day of Muharram. The tazia in different sizes is a work of art, and those made of ivory, sandalwood and silver are not buried but stored for future display.

In *Qadeem Lucknow ki Aakhri Bahar*, an engrossing read of the last days of the monarchy in Lucknow, author Mirza Jafar Husain recounts how the potter Tika Ram built a tazia from clay and people came from far and near to admire the work of the artistic potter.

Notes Aslam Mahmud in *Awadh Symphony*:

> Mirza Jafar Husain also tells us that some of the leading courtesans of Lucknow like Haider Jaan, the two sisters Badr-i Muneer and Mahr Muneer, Bibban, Mughal Jaan, Najja and Hasso sometimes accompanied the tazia processions. However, there was no question of the crowd watching the processions harassing or pestering the women. The roads were decked as if for a fair with

shops of eatables, although by and large the Shia Muslims avoided eating and drinking during the day on Ashura, the tenth day of Muharram. A simple meal was eaten about two hours before sunset.

The tawaifs were provided necessary patronage to innovate their art. The many imambaras in town invited the tawaifs to chant at a majlis, which invariably attracted a large crowd. Everyone wanted to listen to a tawaif at the imambara as it was not possible to visit the tawaif at a majlis hosted by her in her home. The soz renditions by Haidri Jaan were exceptionally enchanting and she attracted large crowds who came not just to listen to her melodious rendition of the marsiya but also to enjoy her pleasant presence.

The tawaif had enjoyed a spiritual connection with many an imambara where patrons encouraged the Urdu text of a marsiya to be composed in local folk tunes and raginis like the bhairavi. The constant confluence of the classical with folk culture made the music preferred during Muharram very popular. The soz compositions are set in ragas that evoke pathos and sung in the khayal style, maintaining at all times the high-pitched vigorous tonal pronunciation of the dhrupad that in better times in Delhi had dominated the marsiya recitations. Green and white clothes were worn by some mourners and none were prevented from participating in the rituals of Muharram that were observed by all citizens.

There was no restriction on the entry of anyone to a majlis and everyone was welcome into the many imambaras, all of which were lit up with countless candles and decorated with replicas of battle flags and other artifacts related to Husain engaged in battle with a cruel dictator. The entire population had participated in this ritual of collective catharsis and shed copious tears at the majlis where the past was forwarded into the present by one poetic repetition of the tragedy of Karbala after another. The sound of people weeping and the rhythm of the beating of the breast by large groups of people, mostly in Shia Muslim homes and at the imambara, had rent the air along with lamentations of mourners expressing distress at the martyrdom of Husain, the younger grandson of Muhammad, the Prophet of Islam. Drums, cymbals and solemn music on streets had accompanied martial art feats by youngsters flaunting clubs and sticks to create a feeling of being in the midst of battle. The gregarious ghazal was replaced by the mourning tone of the marsiya. All doors to the song, dance and drama performances enjoyed throughout the year were shut and assemblies at the *azakhana* or house of mourning were opened.

The frame of mind was reflective even as pageants were prepared and public processions organised on different days of the month. Horses were groomed, palanquins were polished, and the imambara was scrubbed clean and glowed in the light of lamps in coloured glass also displaying many a magnificent tableau of tazia, *alam* and *panja*. Colourful banners and replicas of articles belonging to Husain, like a turban, sword, bow with a quiver of arrows, were laid out in between an army of multicoloured candles and incense sticks.

The Shia Muslim rulers and local artistes collaborated in recreating the incident of Karbala with such creative passion that everyone in Lucknow was able to identify with the tragedy and to empathise with the injustice faced by members of Prophet's family who had sacrificed their lives in order to keep the spirit of Islam alive. Although solemn, Muharram was an aesthetic experience. The imaginative portrayal of suffering of fellow human beings, even so long ago and in such a faraway land, had evoked empathy and stirred up feelings of compassion for others. Presented as tragic drama, the story of Karbala was played out most creatively especially by poets and storytellers and it had a cathartic effect on the population, helping the city to purge itself of suspect emotions.

The rulers of Avadh had followed Shia Islam who believe that the imam complements prophethood. In the absence of the living prophet, the authoritative interpretation of scripture and legitimate legislative powers are conferred to the imam. The imam lends his voice to the silent words of the Quran, making its teachings, instructions and wisdom accessible to devotees. The suffering borne by Imam Husain assures redemption for all humanity and is closely tied to universal salvation. The imam is regarded as an act of divine grace, his role being to lead the faithful through the proper path. It is the imam who intercedes between obvious and cosmic reality. The bearer of the sins of the pious; the martyrs who save their followers who have battled against the army of cosmic ignorance (*al-jahl*) since the origin of creation. The devout encounter divinity through the imam. In mystical terms, 'the historic imamate is fundamentally the religion of love for the face of God, which is none other than the cosmic imam'.

The pious strive to cultivate their inner imam by mourning for Husain and the House of Sorrow. The tears of the pious are believed to be a source of salvation that promise to light up the world and wash away all accumulated injustices suffered by humanity over the ages.

Azadaari is the wait, the *intizar*, for justice, the preparation for collective and individual salvation till forces of intelligence overcome the forces of ignorance for the absolute riddance of injustice and restoration of rightful administration by a just head of government.

In the seventh century, Shia Islam began as a political protest in Persia by a minority group that followed the family of Muhammad, the Prophet of Islam. There was a struggle over succession after the death of the Prophet to the new community of Muslims. The Shia were mostly non-Arabs with grievances against the Arab ruling class. The Shia group was inspired by Ali, closest companion, cousin and son-in-law of the Prophet. The Shia continue to maintain that Ali is the rightful successor to the Prophet of Islam and the leader of the Shia is called imam.

The presence of Shia rulers of Persian origin in Lucknow signalled their political autonomy and provided them an opportunity to bestow a Shia character to the city. Previously they had underplayed their Shia way of life as employees in the Mughal court. In Lucknow the rulers were able to separate their identity from the Sunni Muslim orthodox pressures of the later Mughals and Asaf-ud-Daula found the freedom to build his dream imambara, a Shia institution.

The imambara is not a mosque or a mausoleum. It is built as a house of the imam, the leader. The imambara is unique to South Asia. A structure was built in the eighteenth century in Faizabad by Safdarjung, Asaf-ud-Daula's grandfather, inviting people to assemble to reflect upon the incident of Karbala.

The structure dedicated to Abu Talib, father of Imam Ali, is difficult to locate today, but it was called imambara from *imam* meaning leader in Arabic and *baara* or home in Sanskrit. Even before the grand imambara built by Asaf-ud-Daula, fourth ruler of Lucknow, the heirs of the Mughal rulers of Delhi had constructed probably the first imambara in the city.

After Mughal Emperor Shah Alam was blinded by Ghulam Qadir, a Rohilla warrior, his son and crown prince Sulaiman Shikoh took refuge in Lucknow where Asaf-ud-Daula hosted him with respect and took care of his family. Sulaiman is the grandfather of Bahadur Shah Zafar II, last Mughal emperor, and his mother was a Shia Muslim princess from Persia. While in Lucknow till 1815, Sulaiman Shikoh had hosted mushairas regularly and patronised émigré poets Mushafi, Insha and Jurat. Sikandar, younger son of Sulaiman Shikoh, built an imposing imambara as part of his residential complex in Lucknow in the 1790s.

There was a zenana imambara in the same complex for women who were devotees of Husain. A kitchen had served meals free of cost to the poor adjacent to the imambara. Over time the imambara fell into disuse and functioned as a school for a while till it was demolished, and the grave of Sikandar Shikoh, his wife, and his poet friend Mirza Qateel, who were buried in the same ground, were lost to dust forever.

In Persia, the imambara is called *husainiya* after Husain whose surviving family members felt the need to meet under one roof to repeat injustices that he had faced in Karbala so that his sacrifice was never forgotten. Many husainiya were built in the cities of Aleppo, Baghdad and Cairo from the tenth century, at first as an extension to a mosque. The first meetings of the followers of Husain had taken place in private homes in the seventh century and later imambaras with assembly halls were built for Shia Muslims to meet and to collectively recall the valour and to mourn the martyrdom of Husain in 680 in Karbala.

Centuries later, the inimitable Urdu writer Ismat Chughtai says in *A Drop of Blood*, her last novel, originally titled *Ek Qatra Khoon*, that the 1400-year-old story of Karbala is today's story of about seventy-two people who took a stand against imperialism in order to defend human rights.

Translated into English by Tahira Naqvi, the dedication to Mir Anees, Urdu literature's greatest poet, reads:

> This 1400-year-old story is today's story as well for today too man remains man's worst enemy. For today too, the standard-bearer of humanity is man. Today too, when a Yazid raises his head in some part of the world, Husain steps forward and crushes him, even today light wins against darkness.

Chughtai learnt of the incident of Karbala from the marsiya of Mir Anees, one of Lucknow's most-loved poets, whose long elegy on the battle of Karbala is Urdu literature's greatest treasure. Chughtai, who died in 1991, dedicates her novel from 1976 to Anees because she says she found the story of Karbala in his marsiya. Karbala is of great historical importance and occupies a special place in the religious and cultural life of Shia Muslims. The martyrdom of Husain in 680 has been kept alive by patrons and poets as timeless inspiration for all those people suffering oppression anywhere in the world, at any time. Karbala is presented in Urdu literature as a moment of great courage and daring in the face of cruelty and greed. Wherever innocent people are made to suffer, Husain's sacrifice is remembered. People chant Husain's name whenever they take a stand against injustice and tyranny.

Wajid Ali Shah too built a *baradari* inside the Qaiserbagh palace complex in the 1850s as a house of mourning. The twelve-arched baradari was once called *qasrulaza* or assembly hall for mourning. It was a fashionable place to assemble for a majlis and to together witness the sombre recitation of *sozkhwani*, a dirge with no musical instruments accompanying the recitation. The word *soz* is a Persian word meaning to burn, or passion. It is a performance of three people: the *sozkhwan*, the dirge reciter, the *bazu*, the arm that maintains the *swara*, and the *jawaabi*, the response to the chanting together. This was followed by *marsiyakhwani*, the narration of an elegy, and each majlis ended with the *maatam*, the beating of the chest to a *nauha*, the chanting in a sorrowful raga of a dirge.

All the rituals followed during Muharram are called azadaari, a spiritual exercise in which the entire city had participated. Muharram is festive in its own way and a busy time for musicians, artisans, food vendors and audiences. However, the mood of the city remains contemplative as azadaari is performed. Citizens are no longer playful but philosophical. From humming folk songs, the switch is to the recitation of a dirge, elegy and lamentations composed in sombre raga. This is no time for the mushaira but people assemble at a majlis instead. Professionals would scurry from one majlis to another carrying the marsiya in a cloth bag written by hand on several sheets of paper. The throat was always cleared before the professional began the recitation. The literary flavour of the Muharram spirit among the people of Lucknow in the nineteenth century permeated and touched all levels of society, including the unlettered, and wandering fakirs and beggars solicited alms by reciting verses, like 'May you have no other sorrow except the sorrow of Imam Husain.'

This was a time for all citizens to purge the self of negativity. Crime went down in the city during Muharram. The heart of most citizens was filled with compassion, empathy and love for fellow citizens. Everyone was inspired by emotions that the master *marsiyago* was able to arouse with his dramatic narration of the battle of Karbala for the family of the Prophet.

Almost two centuries later, and in similar spirit, poet Javed Akhtar writes Ansoo, a poem about tears and in praise of mourning. Akhtar seems to suggest in his contemporary poem how the mysterious tear is underestimated. Despite being orphaned, the tear continues its search for stories like Karbala so that it is able to return to its home in the heart of people. Most people have abandoned the tear in order to move on in life without perhaps realising that tears are needed to remind them that they are human. Akhtar, who spent his childhood in Lucknow, says that tears are avoided till someone comes along with a story so sad that the eyelids are again moist.

What is a tear? questions the poet. He adds that the tear is witness to compassion in the human heart and to one's solidarity with other human beings. The tear is proof that a human being is warm and still alive. To tear up means that the heart beats, that listening to the painful story of another human being, the heart is troubled and is lit up by unknown flames. Tears make the heart melt although the sorrowful story is not his own. Where does the tear roll down from? Where was it all this while? Was it always there where it was born? The distance between the heart and the eyelids is where the poet's ideas of life live and dreams are buried. The garden of love, the poet says, has turned into wilderness where only thorns of bitterness are found. Nothing else. Ahead is a thick jungle of anxiety and tears are forsaken after sorrow is slain for the sake of convenience. The tear has none to make it proud. The tear is orphaned. It exists without confidence and lives without direction till a caravan of a sorrowful story passes by, igniting hope in the tear of a home. The tear wishes to be led home by the finger by the friend of sorrow. After asking many a true and false question, the tear makes a tissue of the newly found story so full of sorrow and is overjoyed at the thought of visiting the eyelid of the poet once again.

The round-the-year hustle bustle would intensify during Muharram. Open-air markets kept citizens awake till the wee hours of the morning. The tazia and other mementos precious to people during Muharram were sold under one tent while food stalls put up in every nook and cranny fed the city round the clock.

Aslam Mahmud writes in *Awadh Symphony*:

> Everything that constituted comfort luxury or convenience at normal times was done away with. Ladies no longer used beds and mattresses and lounged on mats on the floor instead. No jewellery to which women were so attached was worn from the time the new moon of Muharram was sighted. Women untied their hair and allowed the tresses to fall in disarray. The colourful attire of the women was replaced by mourning clothes, usually

black, especially during the first ten days of Muharram. Lavish meals were replaced by simple ones. People gave up paan, and any form of entertainment, including music, cinema and games, was stopped.

Many a Hindu citizen had participated in Muharram ceremonies and some wrote mesmerising marsiya. Internalising the pain of Zainab, granddaughter of the Prophet and sister of the martyred Husain, Dilgir describes the house full of happiness that has been wrecked. What destruction is this, he says, and how impossible it is for that family to be joyous again!

Kaisa yeh bhara ghar hua barbaad, ilahi, kya aayi tabaahi
Ab issko naabaad kabhi paiyegi Zainab ghabrayegi Zainab

Channo Lal Dilgir was the brother of Raja Jhau Lal, the kayastha finance minister of Asaf-ud-Daula, fourth ruler of Avadh. Dilgir wrote ghazals at first and took lessons in writing from Nasikh. Once he had discovered the story of Karbala, he tore up all the romantic poetry that he had written earlier to concentrate only on writing marsiya, expressing deep sorrow at the martyrdom of Husain. In another couplet, Dilgir cries over the slaughter of members of the Prophet's family in the battle of Karbala, and without Akbar, Qasim and braveheart Abbas, the freedom of the survivor is worse than captivity.

Akbar hai na Qasim hai na Abbas-e-dilawar
Yeh meri rihaayi toh hai ab qaid se badtar

Fortunately, the world is familiar with Dilgir's writing to this day as it was published by the Nawal Kishore Press in

Lucknow. His work is compiled in six large volumes consisting of about four hundred marsiya which he wrote between 1885 and 1897.

Aslam Mahumud in *Awadh Symphony* says:

> Dilgir's marsiya contain very realistic descriptions of battles. He applauds the adroitness of the sword. His scenes of lamentation are touching. He frequently dwells on the impermanence of the world. He crafted lines like:
>
> *Insaan se hai isi baat ziyad hubab ko*
> A bubble is more constant than a man's life
>
> *Aamaal ke siwa nahin kuchh saath jayega*
> It is only your deeds that will go with you from this world, and
>
> *Kitne hi mehr wa mah zameen mein nihaan hue*
> How many suns and moons that is illustrious people have finally found refuge under the earth?

Dilgir was able to place the characters of the Karbala tragedy within the context of Lucknow society, and the social customs he described were largely local. Scores of other Hindus were inspired to write marsiya. Lal Ram Prashad Bashar even migrated to Karbala and is said to be buried there. Balwan Singh Raja, the son of Maharaja Chait Singh, the ruler of Varanasi, had lived in Agra. He was tutored by Nazeer Akbarabadi, the great Urdu poet who died in Agra in 1830. Lala Har Prashad was an aristocrat and he did not write marsiya, but he was a brilliant narrator. He had followed tazia processions and was much in demand around the city for his recitation of the marsiya written by others. Muslim officials of Hindu rajas had arranged majlis where marsiya written by Mir Anees in Avadhi were recited.

Born in 1882, Pandit Brij Narain Chakbast was impressed with the marsiya of Mir Anees. In his poem *Ramayana*, he writes about Ram's departure into exile in a style similar to that of Mir Anees. Ram bids his father farewell in the name of God. Before he proceeds upon the right path leading to the ultimate destination, he goes to his mother who waits to see him. Ram wipes a tear with the end of his garment. He wonders if seeing him sorrowful, the mother's helplessness will not multiply, only increasing her sorrow.

Rukhsaat hua jo baap se lekar khuda ka naam
Raah-e-khuda mein manzil-e-awwal hui tamaam
Majboor thha jo maa ki ziyaarat ka intezaam
Daaman se ashk pochhke dil se kiya kalam
Izhaar-e-bekasi se sitam hoga aur bhi
Dekha humein udaas toh ghum hoga aur bhi

Mir Anees was a genius when it came to expressing human relationships. The way he described the intimacy of emotions shared by family members is what Chakbast is trying to capture in his own writing. During the battle of Karbala, writes Mir Anees, the women of the family of Husain had wept bitter tears. Bano had stood by in silence, Zainab had prayed for the safety of her nephew Ali Akbar, who was eighteen years old and beautiful to look at. Abbas had held the flagpole and bowed before Husain, his brother. Before going to battle he had touched the feet of Zainab, his sister, who had blessed him and said, 'Brother, I surrender my life to you. Protect me from the heat of battle and bring us peace.'

The word marsiya is Arabic for elegy and its origin is from *risa*, meaning lamentation for the death of a beloved person. In Urdu literature, marsiya implies the versification of the trial of Husain and other members of the Prophet's family and their martyrdom in Karbala. A large number of marsiya were written in the Deccan and in Delhi, but it was in Lucknow that the marsiya gained the magnitude of epic poetry under the patronage of members of the Shia Muslim elite and royalty. It was a popular literary form in ancient Persia and by the time it reached Avadh the marsiya became uniquely localised. In the nineteenth century the images and metaphors used in a marsiya were inspired by the sight and sounds of Avadh.

Nuances of symbols and vocabulary inherited from Persian literature were replaced by more familiar local imageries. In the nineteenth century the Urdu language was exploding with vocabulary borrowed from different languages including from local speech like braj bhasha and avadhi, spoken mostly in the suburbs and heartland of the countryside. Urdu adopted the grammatical structure of the khadi boli and was written in a modified form of the Perso-Arabic script with vocabulary liberally borrowed from Persian and Arabic. This was a moment of a convergence of elite and popular cultures when the urban elite was introduced to folk rhythms and tunes while people on the street got a whiff of classical literary styles.

Musical genres like thumri and dadra from the suburbs of Lucknow fused with the classical raga and hybrid forms of music were created, like the basant ghazal and the sawan ghazal. The aesthetics and emotional content of the ghazal were combined here with seasonal songs to amazing effect. Similar imageries were later used to make sense of Husain's historic battle fought far away and so long ago in Karbala to inspire the Indian freedom struggle. The literati had elevated the incident of Karbala into a poetic metaphor that local people embraced. Karbala was recast in local idiom in such a way that the marsiya touched audiences deeply, making many a poet sigh—if only Husain had come from Medina to India instead! Then River Ganga would have surely been more hospitable to him than the river Euphrates that failed to quench the thirst even of children accompanying Husain.

At least seventeen non-Muslim poets were famous for their marsiya writing, and Malka-e-Zamani, wife of Nasiruddin Haider, the eighth ruler of Avadh, Askari Khatoon and Razia Begum Riasat were three women known for writing the marsiya.

Apart from its emotional content, the marsiya took up intellectual topics like addressing the ideal manner in which a king should rule. In the tradition of the *Mirror for Princes* writings of Europe in medieval times, Mirza Dabir had warned Ghazi-ud-Din Haider, the seventh ruler of Avadh, to beware of practising injustice. Ghazi-ud-Din Haider was impressed by the marsiya and instructed his ministers to never forget Dabir's advice. The Indianised story of Karbala had resonated well with rulers who were forced to think about following the virtuous path of Husain and to avoid the path chosen by Yazid, the ruler of Kufa, whose army had killed Husain.

As the twentieth century approached and the freedom struggle gained momentum, Husain's historic battle became a mirror experience for freedom fighters struggling against British colonialists. Nationalists like Josh Malihabadi, a revolutionary poet born in 1898, gave an intellectual dimension to the marsiya. Josh appropriated the events of Karbala as a timeless example of how to stand up to oppression without fear or pity. Josh had inspired the youth in its ongoing fight for freedom from colonial rule by recalling the battle of Husain in his poetry:

> Josh, call out to Husain, prince of Karbala
> Look at the twentieth century, at the tumult, chaos and the trembling of the earth
> Look at the many yazids today when yesterday there was only one
> In village after village tyranny has appeared again
> And once again the feet of humanity are in chains

This is evident in the elegiac poetry of the modern and the progressive Urdu poets of the early twentieth century. Malihabadi was less emotional and had educated himself to develop a more rational relationship to Karbala. He had discovered *azm-e-husain*, the determination of Husain to bring about a revolution in the Karbala incident. Against the background of colonial rule, it made more sense to Malihabadi to marvel at Husain's will power and determination in times of adversity than to simply lament over Husain's martyrdom.

Malihabadi wrote *Marsia, Husain and Revolution* in 1941 which is considered a superb example of a modern, progressive marsiya rooted in anticolonial thought.

> The historic incident of Karbala has been reinterpreted by poets, updated and modernised to help the socially conscious to deal with oppression in present times.

> Ever since Karbala, the enemy of the people is always addressed as the ruthless Yazid even in successive times. All hypocritical politicians who continue to trouble ordinary populations in modern times are called Yazid while members of the Prophet's family are regarded as the righteous ones. The nobility and the virtuous character of the heroes of Karbala is brought out best by poets who have the power to motivate modern-day societies with their verse to accept the deeds of the historic characters as a contemporary necessity.

Iftikhar Arif was born in Lucknow in 1944 and is an important voice in the world of modern Urdu poetry. Arif is a self-confessed devotee of Husain, and a lover of Mir Anees. Says Arif that Anees has veiled his sorrow with the story of Karbala as he witnessed the helplessness of Lucknow before its takeover by the British. About one particular couplet out of many that he has written about Karbala, Arif says that it is the same thirst, the same desolation, the same household, the same connection of the arrow with a bag of water:

> *Vahi pyaas hai vahi dasht hai vahi gharana hai*
> *Mashkize se teer ka rishta bahut purana hai*

The extraordinary images, metaphors and idioms conjured up in the marsiya, especially by master composer Mir Anees, keep the spirit of Karbala alive, and that alone is a good reason to get to know Mir Anees some more.

Mir Anees

Ashiq ko dekhte hain dupatte ko taankar
Dete hain hum ko sharbat-e-deedaar chhaan kar
'Anees' dam ka bharosa nahin theher jao
Charagh leke kahaan saamne hava ke chale
Ashq-e-gham dida-e-pur-nam se sambhaale na gaye
Yeh woh bachhe hain jo maa baap se paale na gaye
Tamaam umr jo ki hum se be-rukhi sab ne
Kafan mein hum bhi azizon se munh chhupa ke chale
'Anees' aasaan nahin aabaad karna ghar mohabbat ka
Yeh unka kaam hai jo zindagi barbaad karte hain

Peeping at the lover from behind a stretched veil
Offering a goblet of a sieved glimpse
'Anees', life is uncertain, tarry,
Where are you going with a lamp before the wind
Tearful eyes filled with sorrow could do nothing
These are children the parents could not nurture
All my life everyone was indifferent
I too hid from loved ones behind the shroud
'Anees', it is not easy to nurture love's home
This is the job of those who destroy life.

Wajid Ali Shah 'Akhtar'

Ghuncha-e-dil khile jo chaho tum
Gulshan-e-dehr mein sabaa ho tum

Bemuravvat ho bevafa ho tum
Apne matlab ke aashnaa ho tum
Kaun ho kya ho kya tumhein likhein
Aadmi ho pari ho kya ho tum
Pista-e-lab se hum ko quvvat do
Dil-e-bimaar ki davaa ho tum
Ussi Akhtar ke tum hue mashooq
Hanso bolo ussi ko chaho tum

The heart will bloom if you like
In the garden of the world you are the morning breeze
You are faithless, you are inconsiderate,
You are a friend of your own interest
Who you are, what you are, what should I write about you?
Human, fairy—what are you?
Empower me with your pistachio-shaped mouth
Cure of the ailing heart, you are
beloved of Akhtar
Laugh, speak, love, only him.

SEVEN

House of Mourning

Mir Anees was proud of his family and he never forgot to remind his audience that the adoration of Husain remained an age-old tradition in his household. His life, said Mir Anees, had passed in traversing the same terrain and he was the fifth generation to praise Husain. Describing Husain's beauty, Anees writes about his dark curls playing this way and that on a radiant face between earlobes that sparkled like pearls.

Vo gore gore chehron pe zulfein idhar udhar
Akhtar se vo chamakte hue kaan ke guhar

One day Mir Babbar Ali Anees tore up every ghazal that he had ever written in praise of love and the beauty of women—to meditate upon the marsiya. From romantic love, his yearning was to experience one that was mystical. The ghazal and the marsiya are the two most popular forms of Urdu poetry. Like most poets, Mir Anees had flagged off his poetic career by writing ghazals and reciting them at the local mushaira. Even as a thirteen-year-old, Mir Anees had earned much praise for his verses.

Born in a Shia Muslim family in Faizabad, Mir Anees grew up attending majlis and was familiar with the marsiya recited by his elders. He heard Mir Mustahasan Khaliq, his gentle poet father, address assemblies of devotees from the top of the pulpit in the imambara. The story of Karbala was repeated in the style of marsiya during Muharram. Written to mourn the death of a beloved person, the marsiya is a short poem written in praise of someone who is no more. No attention was paid to its literary merit. In Lucknow, Muzaffar Husain Zamir, a contemporary of Mir Khaliq, formalised the way a marsiya should be composed. With Mir Anees, the marsiya attained epic popularity. Towards the end of the eighteenth century, the city blossomed into a centre of a Shia Muslim way of life and developed its own tradition of marsiya writing.

The transformation of marsiya into a lengthy narrative, full of details of the whole story of the battle and the events leading to the martyrdom of Husain, took place mainly in Faizabad and in Lucknow. The best marsiya is filled with exquisite descriptions of local seasons. There are images of nature, social customs and traditions and the different relationships shared within a family. Anees imagines Imam Ali telling sons Hasan and Husain to sit down and not trouble Prophet Muhammad, their grandfather. But Muhammad spreads out his arms and tells the boys, 'Come, come…' Husain asks to be the first one to be cuddled and if Hasan makes it to the grandfather's lap before him, it will make him angry.

Beton ko thha Ali ka ishaara ki baith jao
Laazim nahin ki vaaz mein naana ko tum satao
phaila ke haath bole Muhammad ki aao aao
Shabbir ne kaha humein pehle gale lagao
bhai Hasan jo aapki goadi mein aayenge
Hum tumse naana jaan abhi rooth jayenge

As Mir Anees grew older, he did not just hear but listened to marsiya recitations and began to concentrate on what his father said about Karbala. He thought a great deal about the mystery of death. He tried to figure out the relationship of death to eternity. He contemplated upon ideas of the temporal and the eternal, before he settled down to compose verses. If life is eternal, then it is only the physical destruction of Husain that took place in Karbala and not of the values that Husain practised, he concluded. Mir Anees was convinced that the values Husain stood for, like universal brotherhood, equality amongst all human beings and social justice, are alive even centuries after the death of Husain.

Mir Khaliq was a great teacher and a sensitive poet who felt the grief that he portrayed. His words spoke to the heart of his listeners and the language that he used was simple but attractive. Here Mir Khaliq wishes that the shade of the beloved's tresses had accompanied him to heaven so that he could have enjoyed the garden of paradise even more:

Baagh-e-jannat mein bhi kya khoob guzarti meri
Vahan bhi sar par jo teri zulf ka saaya hota

Mir Anees was proud of his ancestors. His family goes back to Mir Ghulam Husain Zahak whose Iranian ancestors came to Delhi from Herat. For four generations, the family lived in Delhi. Once the decline of the Mughal empire began, the family moved to Avadh. Mir Ghulam Husain Zahak came to Faizabad with his eldest son Mir Hasan and found employment in an office where he compiled proverbs and idioms. He lived in the Gulab Bari neighbourhood where the Anees-o-Chakbast Library is now located. Apart from the marsiya, Mir Ghulam Husain Zahak was famous for his satires and the humorous poetry he wrote.

Mir Khaliq was Mir Hasan's second son and the grandson of Mir Ghulam Husain Zahak. The children were traditionally educated at home even after the family moved to Lucknow. Mir Khaliq had many students and he recommended Nasikh as a teacher for several youngsters who wrote verses. Mir Khaliq had written poetry since he was sixteen years old and it was corrected by Mir Hasan, his father. Mir Hasan is the famous author of *Sihr-ul-Bayan*, an enchanting story in verse which he dedicated to Asaf-ud-Daula. To further refine his verses, Mir Khaliq was sent to Mushafi. Mir Hasan wanted his son Mir Khaliq to learn from Mir Taqi Mir, but the god of poetry said that he did not have time to take more students than he already had.

Mir Khaliq was the last poet in the family to write ghazal after his son Mir Anees decided to compose only marsiya. From Mir Khaliq, Mir Anees picked up proverbs with sophistication. Mir Anees inherited from his father the use of everyday speech in poetry, making it possible for the family's intellectual and artistic river to flow uninhibited and without a break for nearly two and a half centuries. Mir Nafees, a son of Mir Anees and Mir Urooj, a grandson whose son is Mir Faiz, were the eighth generation to perform the art of marsiya.

Mir Anees could not stop thinking about Karbala and was curious to know more about Husain. He wanted to know what Husain the younger grandson of the Prophet of Islam was doing on the banks of the river Euphrates, far away from his home in Medina. The more he thought about the protagonist of the battle of Karbala, the closer he felt to the idea of Husain. An undying love for Husain had made a home in the heart of Mir Anees. The poet concluded that the past is essentially unjust and Muharram is an opportunity for the present to learn from the wrong practised in the past. The purpose of azadaari, the rituals followed during Muharram, was to move towards a cosmic perfection of life that is more equitable than mankind is at present. Ideally, the idea of Husain should inspire one to turn into reality the dream of a better future. That is why Karbala is sacred.

Karbala is sprinkled with the blood of braveheart Husain, making it a place of pilgrimage and of remembrance. The place is eternal witness to the destruction of goodness, and symbolic of hope, of the resurrection of justice, in present times. Husain, the entire house of Muhammad, and all humanity was deprived of justice in Karbala. Karbala had reduced members of the family of Muhammad to a house of sorrow and that is enough reason to never forget Karbala, marking the importance of *zikr* or the remembrance of one's love for values like equality, peace and justice. Karbala is a plea to cherish virtuous morality and all that which benefits not merely individuals, but is crucial and vital to the resolution of every crisis suffered by humanity at large.

In the collective memory of devotees, Karbala cannot be forgotten. The martyrdom of Husain cannot be forgotten. The incident of Karbala encourages selflessness and an alarm bell for society to beware of dictators and usurpers. The remembrance of the martyrdom of Husain, believers say, will keep alive the will of the meek to confront injustices anywhere around the world. The journey is towards finding an equilibrium between cosmic intelligence and cosmic ignorance. Till that happens, poets warn that every day will remain ashura, the tenth day of Muharram, when Husain was killed. Husain could have saved his life and the life of his companions by keeping silent and by doing nothing. But by choosing death in the dark dust storm of Karbala, Husain had lit a lamp so that all humanity could continue its journey on the path of enlightenment.

The traditions of Muharram are meant to facilitate devotees to orient their spiritual life and to reflect upon the historic and undying reality of Karbala. The public display of mourning and the deliberate arousing of sorrow and the shedding of tears amongst devotees is related to the redemptive message of the martyrdom of Husain. The belief is that Husain had known of his violent death and yet he chose to embrace martyrdom in Karbala. That is because Husain felt that martyrdom was necessary at that point in his life and in that moment in history. The need of the hour was to shock humanity out of political slumber and to become aware of the ever-present threat to decency by forces most immoral.

Husain deliberately travelled to Karbala with the women and children of his household so that the world could witness the heartlessness of those in power. He wanted people to recognise those who humiliated and held captive members of the family of Muhammad, the Prophet of Islam, and increase the aversion of the world towards the cruelty of powerful forces in their own times.

Mir Anees personalised the millennium-and-a-half-old tragedy of Karbala for each of his listeners, and felt emotionally enriched by the act. The study of Karbala made his creativity soar. He combined the intensity of grief that he felt at the forceful takeover of Lucknow by the British in 1856 with thoughts of injustices in Karbala. Together the two incidents added heart-wrenching pathos to his writing. The loss of Lucknow to colonialists pained him. His sadness intensified the sorrow he expressed in words over the usurping of the leadership of the community of Muslims from the direct descendants of Muhammad. Those who had once made life impossible for Muhammad when he was alive now strutted around as more pious than the Prophet of Islam.

For Mir Anees, the main purpose of the marsiya was to remind people not only of the sad events of Karbala but also of Husain's courage to stand up to cruelty. His heart was drowned in the parallel he saw between the tragedy in Karbala and in the destruction of Lucknow and its unique way of life by the British. All the love he felt for Karbala and the dislike he nursed for the British came tumbling down in his poetry. Eyewitnesses recall that thousands of men, great and small, would gather to listen to the poetry of Mir Anees, and his audience would go into a trance looking at Mir Anees seated on the pulpit and working his magic over the city with his delightful recitations. Points out Mir Anees that on the battlefield of Karbala, the vision of God is obvious in the desert, every grain of sand up to the peak of the mountain is illuminated by the sun-like face whose light is reflected far and wide:

Dasht-e-vigha mein noor-e-khuda ka zuhur hai
Zarron mein raushni-e-tajalli-e-tur hai
Ik aftab-e-rukh ki ziya dur dur hai

Mir Anees died in Lucknow in 1874 after witnessing how the British had arm-twisted Wajid Ali Shah to grab Avadh and to steal all the wealth of the region. Mir Anees was also witness to the defeat of Lucknow in the war of independence against the British in 1857. The thought that in Lucknow and in Karbala tyranny had triumphed made Mir Anees very sad. It was a thought that was perhaps unbearable to the poet who spent the rest of his life nursing a shattered soul. Mir Anees had moved from Faizabad to Lucknow as a child and had never felt the need to travel elsewhere till the takeover of Lucknow by the British. Mir Anees accepted invites to recite the marsiya in different parts of the country but he was happiest reciting in Lucknow.

'Only the people of this city understand this poetry. What will anyone else know of the worth of the marsiya? And how will he understand the subtlety of our language?' he would say.

The British had reduced Lucknow to a state of utter helplessness but were least respectful towards the traditions of the city. To make a living, Mir Anees went to Allahabad, Hyderabad and Patna after the takeover of Lucknow by the British. In Hyderabad he was offered Rs 10,000 in exchange for the *Lakhnavi* cap that he always wore for a local style. Mir Anees refused, even threatening to not recite the marsiya. He was a man of habit. A trained soldier, Mir Anees practised horse-riding and fencing regularly. He was a tall man with a large moustache and a trimmed beard. He had always dressed meticulously, never stepping out in public without his *angrakha*, a light embroidered robe in muslin cloth and a dome-shaped Lakhnavi cap.

Mir Anees had lost interest in the ghazal early in life to write only marsiya. He composed numerous salaams or salutations to every participant in the battle of Karbala and on the side of Husain. Mir Anees wrote at least ten thousand elegies, reciting as casually as he spoke. The poet gave up writing the ghazal, knowing how popular it was amongst all the other forms of Urdu poetry, including the marsiya, masnavi, qasida and the rubai. Almost three-fourths of Urdu poetry is ghazal as the style allows the poet to enjoy a terrific rapport with the public. The ghazal is able to rise above belief, gender and religion and directly touch the heart of the listener. Even poetry lovers unfamiliar with the Urdu script find it easy to drown in the melody of a great ghazal. This is because the thoughts and feelings are expressed in simple words in a ghazal that are universal and common to all humanity.

Tears well up in the eyes of listeners every time Iftikhar Arif says that his desire is to scatter away like a dream, his existence is so lonesome that he prefers not to exist.

Khvaab ki tarah bikhar jaane ko ji chahta hai
Tanhai itni ki mar jaane ko ji chahta hai

This is the power of the ghazal which makes it a darling of the public and of most poets. In the past, the ghazal was the touchstone of a monarch's court and remains a source of aesthetic and emotional delight for a whole lot of extraordinary and ordinary people. The ghazal is *aabru*, the dignity, of Urdu literature and it has travelled a long way to achieve that pride of place. The story of the oral art of the ghazal is an exciting journey.

It begins from its place of birth in the Arabian Peninsula to the land of the Persians and to Avadh before it made a home in Lucknow where the ghazal has been preserved in writing as well as in print. The Arabic word *taghafful* is the origin of the ghazal, implying the charming act of reaching out and conversing with women who remained mysteriously out of sight throughout medieval times. The absence of women in most societies despite their presence in life mystified the lover who wanted to find out more about the opposite sex. It was the dream of most poets to sit at the feet of the beloved woman in adoration. The poet was confused at the thought that beauties exist in society but are not visible. Why? The poet wants to know in his writing. And that is what poetry is about. It is an expression of the utter confusion experienced by the poet over what is visible in life and what is sensed but invisible. Sahir Ludhianvi brings this sensation down into the twentieth century to wonder how the beloved seems to be everywhere and with everyone, and yet not there; she seems annoyed with the poet but also with herself.

Sab mein shaamil ho magar sab se judaa lagti ho
Sirf hum se hi nahin khud se khafa lagti ho

This poem was used in *Bahu Beti*, a Hindi film released in 1965, where the above lines, sung by Muhammad Rafi to a tune composed by music director Ravi, magnify the helplessness of the poet. The yearning for intimacy with the beloved, the other half of the incomplete self, nags the poet all the time. The anxiety of not being able to ever become whole, never to behold the beloved makes human beings turn to poetry. Powerful feelings of longing turn many into a *majnu*, the feverish lover scorned by society as a crazy man. Society stands like a rock between lovers and is dismissed as the worst enemy of love. For the miserable majnu, the ghazal is his only friend and solace that facilitates him to share his frustration and to talk endlessly of his pain of a lonely existence.

Iftikhar Arif continues that the dreariness of home makes him shudder, but he is not sure why when the day ends, his desire to go home returns:

> *Ghar ki vehshat se larazta hoon magar jaane kyun*
> *Shaam hoti hai toh ghar jaane ko ji chahta hai*

Love was the favourite topic of conversation with women in the past. In the absence of healthy encounters between man and woman, it was easy to fall in love with a shadow, with the whiff of scent, or even with the figment of one's imagination. And verses about many an imaginary experience were written with such unimagined sincerity that listeners accepted what the poet said as absolute truth.

However, Mir Anees was no longer interested in serenading to earthly beauties. His yearning was to move on from romantic to mystical love. Early in his life, he had made Husain his passion, and he was emotionally tuned in to the spiritual symbolism of the incident of Karbala. He composed many a salaam to introduce his audience to all the different characters who were part of the caravan of Husain in Karbala. The salaam is the salutation paid to the companions of Husain at the start of a marsiya. In his recitations, Mir Anees began to compose the salaam in the style of a ghazal. He wrote nauha and quatrains to mourn the martyrdom of Husain, his elegy often running into fifty stanzas lamenting all the while the suffering that the martyrs of Karbala had endured.

In one such nauha—those brief poems seldom more than a dozen verses long, composed in a solemn raga and chanted to rhythm kept with regular beating of the breast—Mir Anees reminds mourners of the fortieth day of the martyrdom of Husain. In the opening verse, the survivors of the Prophet's family have collected at the burial site. They have been released from prison and have returned to the battlefield to lift the corpse of Husain, the grandson of the Prophet. The grave is ready. The women are bareheaded. Fizza, the household help of the family of the Prophet, cries out to Zainab to come as Ali Zain-al-Abedin buries the imam. The joyless Zainab asks that she be buried beside her brother.

The more Mir Anees internalised the meaning of the tragedy of Karbala the more he was inspired to write elegies in praise of Husain. Mir Anees was an ardent devotee of Husain. The poet imagined Husain as an ideal leader who was assassinated by enemies of humanity. With his knowledge of several languages and vast vocabulary, Mir Anees chose poignant words to recite this truth over and over again, arousing unending pathos in the heart of his listeners. Mir Anees asks the beamless sky and wants to know what kind of irony, what kind of justice this is that the same spot on the neck of Husain is favoured by both Shimr and Muhammad. While Muhammad had tickled him with countless kisses, Shimr had struck Husain at the same place on his neck with a sword.

Ae charkh-e-be-madaar yeh kaisa sitam hai aah
Shamsheer-e-shimr aur Muhammad ki bosa-gaah
Jis pe rasool hothon ko malte hon pyaar se
Kat jaaye karbala mein vo khanjar ki dhaar se

The journey of the marsiya follows the same path as the Urdu language. The marsiya was brought to Lucknow from Delhi after it had taken root in the Deccan courts of Muslim rulers, many decades earlier. Under the patronage of the Shia Muslim dynasty in Lucknow, the marsiya witnessed unprecedented popularity and became a quintessential part of the literary and cultural life of the city. The formal but refined language of the nobility of nineteenth-century Lucknow was acclaimed as the epitome of high breeding and manners, and the *zakir*, the narrator, used this language to pepper his recitations with wordplay and original pun. Mir Anees's knowledge was not restricted to Arabic, Persian and Urdu. He was fluent in Avadhi and did a great deal of reading in other local dialects. The style of his mournful verses also takes inspiration from Malik Muhammad Jayasi's *Padmavat* and the storytelling techniques of Tulsidas who wrote the Ramayana in Avadhi. While the influence of the literature written in the Deccan in *dakini* Urdu is well acknowledged, the effect of the *prem margi* narratives of Avadh upon the marsiya have not been studied enough. Mir Anees describes with so much love how the presence of the rose like Hasan and Husain had converted the terrace of the mosque with their sweet scent and laughter.

Masjid mein aaye hanste hue jab voh gul-badan
Khushboo se sehan-e-masjid-e-jaame bana chaman

Mir Anees was equipped with multiple skills and recreated the martyrdom of Husain with vocabulary carefully chosen by him at majlis after majlis in the many imambaras of Lucknow. When Mir Anees addressed a majlis, the streets of the city fell silent, the markets were deserted and homes abandoned as everyone gathered around the *marsiyago.* But Mir Anees was seldom aware of the large crowd that was attracted to him. Once the crowd was so large that the walls of the enclosure where the majlis was being held were torn down to accommodate everyone. On another occasion, watchmen were posted at the entrance. Instructions were given that only poetry-knowing people could attend. The very important citizens of the city were requested to bring no more than two guests with them. However, when it came to listening to Mir Anees, the crowd was never in the mood to obey rules. It was deaf to what the watchmen said and insisted on an audience with Mir Anees. Doors were broken down and listeners almost always found at least standing room. The voice of Mir Anees was powerful that even those sitting farthest away from him could hear every word that he spoke.

When he was praised as a great poet, Mir Anees replied, 'What poet? I only share with you a story full of sorrow.'

Mir Anees invariably began his recitations with a prayer for the prosperity of the family of the Prophet. The master marsiyago and ace performer would measure every word that he spoke. He used local similes and metaphors in Urdu instead of Persian cultural symbols. The poet wishes that the family of the Prophet may bud, bloom and may forever remain evergreen, the married life of the women be as fragrant as sandalwood and their arms never empty of children:

Yaar ab rasool-e-paakki kheti hari rahe
sandal se maang bachhon se goadi bhari rahe

The audience invariably responded with groans of appreciation at the drama Mir Anees was able to create with words. Mir Anees had been charming audiences since he was very young. It had now become a habit with him to mesmerise listeners with his presence as well as his recital. It was impossible for the audience gathered in the hall of mourning to look away from the apparition before them. Mir Anees sat high up on a pulpit that was covered in a sheet of black cloth. Against the dark background of the pulpit, the presence of Mir Anees in a snow-white dress sparkled brighter than a star on a moonless night. The long, flowing angrakha worn by him was fashioned with delicate embroidery on gossamer-fine muslin cloth. The attire was matched with a five-cornered cap placed on his head at an angle. The cap was also cut of the same embroidered material in sparkling white. Around him were all the decorations inside the imambara, the fluttering flags and battle crests. The tabernacle had several chandeliers held up with lustrous support. Prismatic crystals and coloured glass shone with flames that had lit up the premises where a raised platform displayed tomb-like structures in filigree, some eight to ten feet high and studded with precious stones. Banners of the rulers of Avadh were hoisted beside replicas of the battle flags of Husain embroidered with verses from the Koran in gold and covered in sheets of fresh flowers. Talismanic words, sacred reminders like lances and turbans of companions of Husain along with a real horse splattered in red colour, and wooden imitations of Zuljana, the horse that Husain took to battle in Karbala, were seen at every imambara.

Hai kahan hai mera bhai ae Zuljana

Here, Zainab, Husain's sister, questions the horse when he returns to her without its rider: where is my brother, oh Zuljana!

Everyone wanted to listen to Mir Anees because his writing was peerless and his recitation beyond compare. He was admired for his voice that perfectly matched his height and his expressive face. The fragrance of seasonal flowers had floated in the air mingled with the sweat of people seated shoulder to shoulder with each other for hours. Whiffs of rose water, vetiver and fragrant smoke from incense sticks accompanied the solo voice of the marsiyago whose recitations were answered with cries of sorrow, deep sighs and constant sobbing by the mourners.

Queen Malika Kishwar, mother of Wajid Ali Shah, was an admirer of Mir Anees and often a part of the audience. She would attend the majlis accompanied by a large entourage and listen to the marsiya recitation of Mir Anees in pin-drop silence. The Queen Mother sat surrounded by companions inside the women's enclosure at the royal house of mourning. Sometimes Mir Anees began his recitation by describing the body of the martyred Husain, heightening the emotions of his listeners. In his recitation, Mir Anees counted nineteen hundred wounds of sword, lance and axe on the body of the grandson of the Prophet that had transformed into a rose, and turned the burning sands of Karbala into a tulip garden. The imagery of the rose, tulip, nightingale and garden is mystical vocabulary borrowed from Sufi poetry written in Persian where the early morning breeze from the east looks for the beloved creator of the world in the rose garden on earth. On the tongue of the nightingale in the same garden of life, there is no other talk except of the same beloved. The splendour of the beloved's creativity is displayed in every colour, and whichever flower is visited, its aroma is the same as that of the beloved.

From the top of the pulpit Mir Anees described how the divine presence of Husain had transformed the desert sands of Karbala into paradise. In the midst of insufferable heat and the most appalling thirst, the blood of Husain had painted the desert green, turning it into a garden planted with a luxuriant row of trees where nightingales sang, perched upon roses soaked in dew.

The tradition is to collectively listen to marsiya during Muharram in the company of numerous other devotees of Husain who enjoy the exaggerated wordplay and puns, presented by the poet. The narrative by an accomplished zakir has the power to dazzle devotees whose solidarity with the story of sorrow helps individual emotions to boil over. The marsiya talks about the plight of little children suffering from the heat and cruelly murdered by arrows hurled at them by the heartless enemy. The recitation of Mir Anees in simple Urdu was emotive and succeeded in making the audience accept the pain of another as its own. The women who were part of Husain's caravan in Karbala are made to speak in colloquial Urdu like a chiding mother or a grief-stricken sister in real life.

Pathos was created with words chosen ever so carefully and which rarely failed to evoke genuine tears and sincere exclamations of grief even among people who did not know how to read or write. It is not unusual for those without formal education to know the marsiya of Mir Anees from memory. The range of vocabulary of Mir Anees was vast and collected over time from having participated in majlis from childhood and from growing up in a family of poets filled with piety. Mir Khaliq had educated Mir Anees and prepared him thoroughly before the son was allowed to take over the pulpit from the father.

It was in this environment that Mir Anees and Mirza Salamat Ali Dabir emerged as two major composers of marsiya in Lucknow. To this day, Muharram, marsiya and Mir Anees are spoken of in the same breath.

In his book titled, *Shia Muslims of India: Religion, Society and Culture*, author Nadeem Hasnain writes:

> Not only his poetry, he was also a great performer who could mesmerise the audience with his language as well as style of presentation. Even Ghalib showered praise on him again and again for his poetry. His amazing language drew vocabulary from Arabic, Persian, Urdu, Hindi and Avadhi. He is unparalleled in whatever he described from nature, animal, human relations, loyalty and even war and weaponry. It is said that no other Urdu poet or writer has used the vocabulary as large as in his poetry and his style of recitation made his audience and readers feel as if they were present on the scene of action.

Here Mir Anees says in praise of his own eloquence that his oratory is the salt upon the food of thought:

> *Namak-e-khwaan-e-takallum hai fasaahat meri*

Mirza Dabir never wrote a ghazal in his life and was best at writing marsiya. He was born and brought up in Delhi around the same time that Mir Anees was born in Faizabad in 1802. Lucknow had welcomed Mirza Dabir with open arms and was proud of his devotion to azadaari. Mirza Dabir has left at least three thousand elegies. And together Mir Anees and Mirza Dabir raised marsiya writing to heights that often seem to surpass that of the ghazal.

Lucknow had all this and much more to offer in those days. Citizens had at their disposal song, dance, drama, poetry and sports; yet the temperament of the people of Lucknow was such that it was ever ready for more fun and games. The city was steeped in excess in every walk of life and had no practice of knowing when to admit that enough is enough. The city was so used to being entertained non-stop that apart from cock fights, quarrels between citizens were also concocted in hope of a little more fun. After having enjoyed the spectacle of rivalry between the poets Mushafi and Insha, and Aatish and Nasikh in the past, the idle lot of Lucknow orchestrated a battle of insults between the followers of Mir Anees and Mirza Dabir as well.

At first, brother was made to quarrel with brother. Mir Anees was the eldest of three brothers and all of them were poets. Sycophants had whispered that Mir Munis, the younger brother, is praised for his recitations only because his verses are first corrected by Mir Anees.

'The day he recites an elegy without you looking over it, the whitewash will peel away,' a voice had whispered to Mir Anees, making sure that the hostility between the brothers was kept simmering. Mir Anees was mild of manners and tried his best to resist falling into the trap laid out by countless mischief-makers around town.

Mir Anees loved his brothers. It was his habit to recount

to and rehearse with his brothers before a public performance. A mirror was used to polish their act and to keep an eye on weaknesses of their craft. All three of them would disappear into a room and in front of the mirror they would perform, noting down expressions, gestures and pauses. They would discuss with each other the best possible style to adopt that would enhance communication with the audience. Mir Anees wanted to get the message of Karbala across to as many people as possible in order to inspire them to follow in the courageous footsteps of Husain. He wanted his recitations to make a lasting home in the heart of each one who listened to him. That is the reason he worked very hard to win over the audience with emotionally charged verses about family members being separated from each other or facing opponents fearlessly. He made Nature participate in his narrations, making it respond to circumstances surrounding the protagonist, pointing out to birds that sailed across the sky and the deer grazed in the grassland while the lion of the forest roared on the banks of the river.

Taair hawa mein mast hiran sab zazar mein
Jangal ke sher goonj rahe thhe kachhar mein

Both Mir Anees and Mirza Dabir had admired each other's art and were always polite to each other. It was their respective flunkeys who had disgraced themselves with the sport of insulting each other in public.

From the book *Lucknow: Memories of a City*, in a chapter titled 'Urdu in Lucknow and Lucknow in Urdu', authors C.M. Naim and Carla Petievich write that one prominent feature of the literary milieu that emerged in Lucknow in the nineteenth century was furious public displays of rivalry between poets.

> Rivalry among poets was always a prominent feature of literary life in the pre-modern days. Its causes lay in the institutions of mushaira, etymologically the word implies contestation, and courtly patronage as well as in the fact that pre-modern poets regarded themselves as men with a profession. In Lucknow, in contrast to Delhi and the Deccan, we find such rivalry taking on the proportions of processions and street fights. Was this a matter of higher stakes, or was it some personal inclination of the patrons that encouraged the poets to display their rivalries in the streets of Lucknow? Perhaps it was a matter of both further enhanced by a prevalent taste in public entertainment in the form of such contests or fights as kite flying, cock fights, quail fights and mock abusive quarrels between low-caste women.

The mischievous made sure that encounters between the partisans of Mir Anees and Mirza Dabir did not end.

If the followers of Mir Anees praised the limpid style of the master's speech, his beauty of description and picturesque idiom, the fans of Mirza Dabir were quick to point out the grandeur of his words and the freshness of theme. Mirza Dabir's eloquence was unacceptable to the Aneesian who found in his verses a blade of grass after digging up a mountain. The Dabirian replied that Mir Anees was capable of nothing except hot air and mere wagging of the tongue. The Aneesian said that his power of description is beyond doubt and his simplicity unobtainable. The engaging eloquence of Mir Anees is a natural gift and it does not come merely from reading books or blackening pieces of paper with ink.

Mere pomp and show of words are good for nothing, said one side, to which the other side replied in praise of the fertile temperament of its hero. Mir Anees learnt the art of marsiyagoi from his elders from one breast to another and that is why he knows how to do his job best. Mirza Dabir did not belong to a learned family of poets. His father worked for a paper merchant and his admirers made it loud and clear that he did not need the combined advice of his elders or of his siblings to be able to write the way he did. That is why the Aneesians said that the many stanzas composed by Mirza Dabir remain disconnected and are full of faults. His similes are defective and the metaphors improper.

This way both sides continued to hurl abuse at each other to the glee of their giddy audience. The more sensible ones concluded that both Mir Anees and Mirza Dabir are superb. While one is the sun, the other is the moon. Sometimes this one is the sun and the other one the moon, and sometimes that one is the sun and this one the moon. Both possessed a certain power that made listeners weep, or laugh at will. The arrangement of words and ideas used by both was such that they were able to enchant and to make the audience sit in stony silence or burst into vivacity. Here Mirza Dabir is at his grandiose best when he writes, 'Don't call it the sun for it was a blot on the breast of dawn, the light of hope for the family of the Prophet is withdrawn':

Kahiye na mehar subah ke seene pe daagh thha
Ummeed-e-ahal-e-bait ka ghar becharaagh thha

Mirza Dabir was a student of Mir Muzaffar Husain Zamir, a contemporary of Mir Khaliq, who was the father of Mir Anees.

Mirza Dabir was a restless child and drawn to piety. As he got older, he realised that he did not want to do anything else in life except compose marsiya. Mirza Dabir had no interest in worldly matters, and he never wrote a single ghazal. While still young, Mirza Dabir was annoyed at the way Mir Zamir had corrected his verse. He went to the elderly Nasikh to show him his verse and to complain about his teacher. As usual, Nasikh was holding court in his inner yard. He sat resting against cushions and was busy talking to visitors who surrounded him when Mirza Dabir voiced his annoyance. Said Mirza Dabir, 'Sir, in this verse I had used this word this way but my ustad has replaced it with this correction.'

'Your ustad is correct,' replied Nasikh and continued the conversation that Mirza Dabir had interrupted.

'Sir, but in books it is written in the way I wrote it,' Mirza Dabir said.

'No. What your ustad has corrected is proper,' Nasikh responded patiently.

Mirza Dabir refused to be quiet. He continued, 'But, but, but … Sir, it is here in this book. Please just look at this book,' and adamantly pulling out a book he tried to show it to Nasikh.

Nasikh was furious. He had lost his patience.

'What! What do you know about books? You present books in my presence. I have looked at so many books that I have become a book myself,' thundered the elderly poet.

Nasikh was so angry that he picked up a cane standing nearby and got up. Mirza Dabir spun around like a top and decided to flee. Nasikh chased him for a while before returning to sit back against the cushions in the courtyard and to continue to talk about poetry.

After the defeat of Lucknow by the British, the garden of poets was turned into wilderness and a lot of literary work done in the city for nearly a century was lost to the wind in the loot that accompanied the 1857 war against the British.

Despite the loss, a little still remains of Lucknow's poetic legacy left by the likes of Mir Anees that continues to inspire contemporary Urdu poets like Lucknow-born Iftikhar Arif. This poet has taken the metaphor of Karbala and freed it from the confines of the faith of a single community. Arif's Karbala is a space that is relevant today to all of humanity. Arif writes, 'Husain, you are no more, your family is no more, but after your martyrdom, the fear of tyrants is also no more.'

Husain tum nahi rahe tumhara ghar nahi raha
Magar tumhaare baad zaalimon ka darr nahin raha

Many find it impossible to get over the horror of Karbala where the family of the exalted lineage of Muhammad, the Prophet of Islam, is left to die of thirst in the burning hot sands of desert waste. (The children of the same Muhammad who had spent his entire life humanising the harsh and miserable life led by the Arabs of the Hijaz in pre-Islamic Arabia, are made to suffer). For all those who know about Karbala even a little, it is difficult to digest the extent of shame, wretchedness and dishonour that the family of Muhammad was exposed to in Karbala. 'How dare you?!' The lovers of Husain have not tired of questioning those who usurped the leadership of the community from Husain and who were cruel and hostile to Muhammad before the Prophet's final success in Mecca. The tragedy of Karbala and the martyrdom of Husain, grandson of the Prophet, affects all aspects of life of devotees, but it seems to have fired the imagination of the literati the most. The historic injustice inspires marsiya writing like no other genre of poetry, and poets continue to write about Karbala as passionately as Mir Anees. But the religious content of the marsiya also restricts its reach to a larger audience in comparison to the very secular content of the ghazal. With repeated calls to humanity to invest more time in appreciating and loving each other, the ghazal was able to melt even the most hardened of hearts.

Here Wajid Ali Shah begs to be loved as love will surely make a human being out of him. In return for love, will he have to surrender his faith and his god? The poet asks in a more playful tone of voice:

Mohabbat se banda bana lijiyega
Bataa dijiye kya khuda lijiyega

The central theme of love in Urdu poetry set lovers' heart on fire, beyond boundaries and irrespective of religion, caste, class and creed. It reinforced the belief that all that there is to life is love. Urdu itself is a result of love, a great attraction of the classical languages of Persian, Sanskrit and Prakrit to the local dialects of avadhi, braj bhasha and khadi boli. Eventually the vocabulary and grammar of all these mediums of communication married to give birth to a brand-new language. Urdu is a miracle. Within a short span of less than a century, a language surfaced dripping in lyricism. Every heart that crossed the path of Urdu was drowned in its musicality. Urdu had inherited musicality from the earthy metaphors and idioms picked up from the many dialects spoken by people in the heartland of Avadh and in the countryside on the western border of the province with Delhi.

Urdu is able to explore the enigma of life in sing-song recitations similar to the way the avadhi dialect is spoken and to the rat-a-tat rhythm of braj bhasha. While the Arabic and Persian speech is formal and grand, the vocabulary taken from Sanskrit and the folk languages is personal and colloquial. Here Aatish uses the colloquial *teri* (yours) instead of the formal *aap* (you) to praise the beloved and to say that your beauty is such that other beauties matter not much:

Ajab teri hai ae mehboob soorat
Nazar se gir gai sab khubsoorat

The informal but earnest cry of the poet longing for love is the charm of Urdu. Urdu is so expressive in its feelings that it connects with listeners instantly, making each one feel enriched with a more wholesome sense of self. To this day a fascination with Urdu continues not only in Lucknow but worldwide. About a billion people speak the language in different parts of the globe and many universities teach Urdu. However small, the community of Urdu speakers are happy to be led through the weft and the warp of Urdu poetry with its promise of a glimpse of eternity at the turn of, one is never sure, which verse.

It is its obsessive theme of love that raises Urdu to a pinnacle. Urdu is preoccupied with a love that blossomed from the intermingling of Hindu and Muslim thought. It was circumstances that had brought a bouquet of people professing different religions and from different corners of the world to spend time with each other. In the bargain, a common language evolved amongst people who did not have only religion on their mind. Some Muslims learned Hindi like the Sufi poet Malik Muhammad of Jaisi who wrote *Padmavat* in verse in the sixteenth century in Avadh in the time of Mughal Emperor Humayun. *Padmavat* is a local legend of love, heroism and sacrifice. At the same time there were surely multitudes of Hindus who had knowledge of Persian and over time a cosy compromise between the different languages resulted in the birth of Urdu.

The word Urdu is a Turkic word for army camp and the origin of the English word 'horde'. Here horde refers to a continuous line of warriors of Central Asian origin who galloped down the Pamir mountains to conquer a large part of the world, including South Asia. However, the influence of the Turkic languages is minimal upon Urdu, perhaps because the Turkic hordes had paused in lands influenced by the lifestyle of Persian conquerors before they continued their journey to make a home in the Gangetic plains. It will not be wrong to say that Urdu is a Persianised form of the language spoken in urban areas of Avadh and by ordinary people living on the border between Avadh and Delhi. The grammar remains Hindi and the vocabulary is a mix of Sanskrit, Hindi, Arabic and Persian.

After the Muslim conquest of South Asia, the local language of a large part of north India was infiltrated with Arabic and Persian words. Traders from all over the world, adventurers and holy men had already introduced vocabulary from their respective language into different Indian languages much before the arrival of Islam.

Exactly when Urdu became Urdu and the local dialects were lumped together under the name of Hindi is difficult to say. The evolution of Urdu began even before the rule of north India by Muslim Turkic warriors in Delhi in the early thirteenth century as Arabs and Persians were in and out of South Asia for centuries before the military conquests by Muslims. A dialogue between all the different influences eventually culminated into a language that came to represent a high culture as it received generous patronage from the rulers of the time.

Melody is at the heart of Urdu. Like all oral traditions anywhere in the world, the importance of recitation was already well developed in India. The rhythm, musicality and lyricism of the local style of recitals, and the joyful combination of sense to sound was picked up by Urdu as well. Urdu poets were aware of how sensitive the classical poets were to sound as reflected in the verses of none other than Kalidas from the fifth century. The most lyrical of all the poems of the Sanskrit poet remains *Meghaduta* (the cloud messenger).

In a 2021 English translation, poet and editor Abhay K. looks at *Meghaduta* through a contemporary lens.

> Like the slender arms of the lady river, Vaanira branches reach out to take away her water garment and expose her thighs, the banks. O friend, of course it would take long for you to depart, for who has the strength to leave a woman after relishing her bare thighs?

Originally written in the slow-paced *mandakranta* metre in 120 stanzas, the poem by Kalidas is a soulful cry of a lover separated from the beloved. The lover pleads with a passing cloud to take his message of love to the beloved. The poetic conceit of the poem rests on *viraha*, the expression of the pain of the lover's separation from the beloved. The local sentiment of the viraha is similar to the angst-ridden experience in the Islamic world of *hijr*, also separation. The idea of hijr is a central theme in Urdu poetry as a dramatic contrast to *vasl* or unity with the beloved. In the third quarter of the twentieth century, Iftikhar Arif finds it ironic that in the heat of separation, there is talk of shade:

Hijr ki dhoop mein chhaon jaisi baatein karte hain...

Later all these poetic traditions must have been on the mind of Rabindranath Tagore as well as he wrote *Gitanjali*, a collection of spiritual lyrics, in 1912.

The same stream of life that runs through my veins
night and day runs through the world and dances in
rhythmic measures.

I feel my limbs are made glorious by the touch of this
world of life. And my pride is from the life-throb of
ages dancing in my blood at this moment.

By the time the nineteenth century ended, Urdu was completely indigenised. The language was loaded with colloquial expressions, and its concern was the common experience of people here. The generously inclusive soul of Urdu had piled up an enviable wealth of vocabulary with which poets had a field day exploring different aspects of life—from spirituality to sensuality. Poets found the freedom to play down romantic love and to flirt with the revolutionary potential of the language. The cry for a revolution against colonialism was heard in Urdu, and poverty, illiteracy and the predicament of the underprivileged universalised in the writings in Urdu.

Raghupathi Sahai was born in 1896, in an affluent family of Hindu landlords in Gorakhpur, which was further east from Lucknow. His family was famous in the area as the Kayastha lords of five villages.

When Sahai began to compose poetry, he adopted the pen name of Firaq Gorakhpuri, and over time he learnt to express complex emotions in simple vocabulary. *Firaq* means distance in Urdu, and the English Literature graduate from Allahabad University was a great fan of the poems of William Wordsworth whose influence on Firaq is obvious. Like Wordsworth, Firaq includes aspects of nature in his romantic writings. The poet asks who is it that stretches, making the heavens drowsy:

Kaun yeh le raha hai angdaai
Aasmaanon ko neend aati hai

Firaq is one of the most-loved poets of present times for saying simple things like, the heart is here, loneliness is here, it would be nice if you were here as well:

Main hoon dil hai tanhai hai
Tum bhi hote achha hota

Firaq died in 1982 after having put his finger to the quintessentiality of Urdu. The beauty of Urdu is the lyricism inherited from the many folk languages that gave birth to it. Urdu is well equipped to handle a gamut of emotions and is a storehouse of inherently musical expressions. With the ease of one who had mastered the language, Firaq asks to be understood when he says that love is divine grace and not a sin.

Koi samjhe toh ek baat kahun
Ishq taufiq hai gunah nahin

To his dying day in 1982, Firaq wondered at his own ability to bring alive the emotion of love by giving it a human body. Urdu allowed him to explore his relationship to life and to the universe through that lone idea of love. Poets marvel at the power of Urdu to encourage endless reflection upon the world as well as upon personal values. Firaq was a poet and a philosopher. He had little time for religion but was deeply rooted in his culture, of which Urdu was his strongest strength. It did not matter to Firaq that he was born in a Hindu family while one parent of the Urdu language was Persian, the mother tongue of the Iranian people who are Muslim.

When Nawab Mirza Khan Dagh Dehlvi died in 1905, Firaq was barely ten years old. Unlike other poets including Mir Taqi Mir, Dagh Dehlvi did not migrate to Lucknow. He had visited Lucknow but never lived here for any length of time. Dagh was born and brought up in the red fort of Delhi where his mother was married to prince Mirza Mohammad Sultan, son of Bahadur Shah Zafar, the last Mughal emperor. After the fall of Delhi in 1857, Dehlvi travelled to Rampur and to Hyderabad, where he died. And the language travelled around the world with similar poets and wandering adventurers to melt the heart as well as make thoughts sit up straight. What makes the name Urdu a cut above the rest only Dagh knows, said the poet, as praise for his language echoes all over Hindustan:

Urdu hai jis ka naam humin jaante hain 'Dagh'
Hindostan mein dhoom hamaari zabaan ki hai

Poets born after Dagh continue to agree that Urdu is indeed praiseworthy. Urdu is unique because almost in a flash, a smattering of *boli* or dialects had bonded together to emerge into a full-fledged *bhasha* or language that is able to fulfil the emotional and intellectual needs of both the poet and the audience. Poets find in Urdu endless freedom to take a subjective poem and to dress it up in universal significance. The poet may interpret a personal experience but is simultaneously able to express deeply felt universal truths in attractive vocabulary arranged in the best possible order.

Urdu was born of change and of evolution. The language still encourages those who love it to keep wiping the dust that invariably creeps into every aspect of life over time, and whenever the language falls into slumber to polish it with the magic still left. Perhaps like today?

Today the eighty-year-old, Lucknow-born Iftikhar Arif is ridden with angst as he regrets that no one from that golden age remains. From where he comes, nothing of anyone remains. To trace with love dreams of those days, I am still around, but after me no one remains, he says. When questioned what is beyond, twinkling, the stars replied, love of my life, there is nothing:

Muhaafiz-e ravish-e raftagaan koi nahin hai jahaan ka
Main hoon mera ab wahan koi nahin hai

Guzishta gaan-e-mohabbat ke khvaab likhne ko
Abhi toh main hoon badezaan koi nahin hai

Sitargaan se jo poochha ke uss taraf kya hai
Chamak-ke bole ae jaanejaan koi nahin hai

Acknowledgements

Rashmi Menon at Amaryllis, Manjul Publishing House, and her patience is the one reason why you hold this book in your hand today. Thank you, Rashmi, for waiting for the manuscript beyond several deadlines.

Thank you, Bidisha Srivastava, my editor, for cleaning up the text with so much love. Thank you, Wasim Helal, for the wonderful cover.

Kanishka Gupta, my literary agent, thank you for finding me a fine publishing house like Amaryllis.

I would like to thank Iftikhar Arif, Professor Anisur Rahman, Noor Zaheer, Saif Mahmood, Salim Arif and Timsal Masud for contributing to the book despite the hectic schedule they keep.

Thank you, Iftikhar Arif, for the Foreword and for talking to me endlessly about Lucknow and Urdu poetry as I wrote the book. It is a matter of great pride for me to have the first draft of the book read by Iftikhar Arif, a Lucknow boy and a living legend of Urdu poetry.

Words are my only legacy for Jaffar and Ali. Thank you, sons, for your inspiring presence in my life.

Last but not the least, I would like to thank every reader who has shown interest in reading about a bygone world where those in power had once felt morally inspired to practise the golden rule of treating others the same way they had wanted to be loved and treated themselves.

—Mehru Jaffer
Lucknow, 2023

Bibliography

1. *Aab-e-Hayat* by Muhammad Husain Azad, originally published in 1880.
2. *Beloved Delhi: A Mughal City and Her Greatest Poets* by Saif Mahmood, New Delhi: Speaking Tiger, 2018.
3. *The Hidden Garden: Mir Taqi Mir* by Gopi Chand Narang and Surinder Deol, New Delhi: Penguin, 2021.
4. *Memory of Light* by Ruth Vanita, New Delhi: Penguin, 2020.
5. *A Thousand Yearnings: A Book of Urdu Poetry and Prose*, edited by Marion Molteno and translated by Ralph Russell, New Delhi: Speaking Tiger, 2017.
6. *Wanderers, Kings, Merchants: The Story of India Through Its Languages* by Peggy Mohan, New Delhi: Penguin, 2021.
7. *Mir Taqi Mir: Selected Poetry*, translated into English by KC Kanda, New Delhi: Sterling Publishers, 1997.
8. *Poetry of Belonging: Muslim Imaginings of India 1850–1950* by Ali Khan Mahmudabad, New Delhi: Oxford University Press, 2020.
9. *Ghalib: A Wilderness at My Doorstep* by Mehr Afshan Faruqi, New Delhi: Penguin, 2021.

Appendix

1. Mirza Muhammad Rafi 'Sauda' (1713–1781)

Couplets

Jab yaar ne utha kar zulfon ke baal baandhe
Tab maine apne dil mein laakhon khayaal baandhe

When the beloved lifted the tresses to lock
then my heart found endless thoughts to lock.

Kaifiyat-e-chashm usski mujhe yaad hai 'Sauda'
Saagar ko mire haath se liijo ki chala main

The look in her eyes I recall, 'Sauda'
Now take the glass from the hand as I am on my way.

Na kar 'Sauda' tu shikva humse dil ki bekaraari ka
Mohabbat kis ko deti hai miyaan aaraam duniya mein

No, 'Sauda', don't complain about the restless heart
Who has found joy in love, my friend?

Fikr-e-maash ishq-e-butaan yaad-e-raftagaan
Iss zindagi mein ab koi kya kya kiya kare

Concern for bread and butter, love of idols,
remembering those who are no more
Now how much more can be done in this life!

Gila likhun main agar teri bewafai ka
Lahu mein garq safina ho aashnaai ka

If I lament your treachery in writing
the ship of friendship will be drowned in a sea of blood.

2. Mir Taqi Mir (1723–1810)

Ghazal

Main kaun hoon ae hum-nafasaan sokhta-jaan hoon
Ik aag mere dil mein hai jo shola-fishaan hoon
Laaya hai mera shauq mujhe parde se baahar
Main varna vahi khalvati-e-raaz-e-nihaan hoon
Jalva hai mujhi se lab-e-dariya-e-sukhan par
Sad-rang meri mauj hai main tab-e-ravaan hoon

Panja hai mera panja-e-khurshid mein har subah
Main shaana-sifat saaya-e-ru zulf-e-butaan hoon
Dekha hai mujhe jin ne so deewana hai mera
Main bais-e-aashuftagi-e-tab-e-jahaan hoon
Takleef na kar aah mujhe jumbish-e-lab ki
Main sadd sukhan-aaghushta-ba-khoon zer-e-zabaan hoon
Hoon zard gham-e-taaza-nihaalaan-e-chaman se
Uss baagh-e-khizaan-dida mein main barg-e-khizaan hoon

Rakhti hai mujhe khvaahish-e-dil bas-ki pareshaan
Darpai na ho is vaqt khuda jaane kahaan hoon
Ik vahm nahin besh meri hasti-e-mauhum
Uss par bhi teri khaatir-e-nazuk pe garaan hoon
Khush-baashi-o-tanziya-o-taqaddus thhe mujhe 'Mir'
Asbaab pade yoon ki kai roz se yaan hoon

Who am I, my fellow human beings, but inflamed by passion I am
There is a fire in my heart, a restless inferno I am
My yearning has unveiled me
otherwise I remain the same recluse I am
Charisma on the shore of the river of poetry is because of me, but
by nature, colourful are my emotions, easygoing I am
My fist like the paw of the sun every morn
reveals faces and tresses of idols, like light I am
Whoever knows me is crazy about me
The cause of all distraction in the world I am
Don't bother, alas, to move the lips
the tongue of poetry dipped in blood I am

I am pale like grief in a nursery of fresh blossoms
In the garden of waste like an autumn leaf I am
The desire of the heart has me worried
Want is misplaced as God knows this moment
where I am
No doubt my imaginary life is an extravaganza
Above all for your pleasure unpleasant I am
Cheerful, funny and purity was said to be Mir
All that had once belonged to me is somewhere,
and here I am.

Dekh toh dil ki jaan se uthta hai
yeh dhuan sa kahaan se uthta hai
Gor kis diljale ki hai yeh falak
shola ik subah yahaan se uthta hai
Khaana-e-dil se ziinhaar na ja
koi aise makaan se uthta hai
Naala sar kheenchta hai jab mera
shor ek aasmaan se uthta hai
Ladti hai uski chashm-e-shok jahaan
ek aashob vaan se uthta hai
Sudh le ghar ki bhi shola-e-awaaz
duud kuchh aashiyaan se uthta hai
Baithne kaun de hai phir usko
jo tir-e aastaan se uthta hai
Yun uthe aah uss gali se hum
jaise koi jahaan se uthta hai
Ishq ek 'Mir' bhaari patthar hai
kab yeh tujh naa-tavaan se uthta hai

Watch it rise from the hearth of the heart. From where else does this smoke arise?
What soul is buried here that flames the sky every morning with rising envy?
Beloved, leave not the heart, does anyone abandon a home like this?
When the head held up high implores, restlessness rises in heaven.
When the wandering look of the beloved clashes with another, tears arise.
Your fury and your fire will burn down the dwelling, there is smoke rising from the home.
Who else will entertain the one turned away from your doorstep.
Who returns once risen from your doorstep when I leave the lane of the lover, a sigh rises like a farewell to life.
Love, Mir, is heavy as a stone; it is not for a weakling like you.

Patta patta boota boota haal humaara jaane hai
Jaane na jaane gul hi na jaane baagh toh saara jaane hai
Aage uss mutakabbir ke hum khuda khuda kiya karte hain
Kab maujood khuda ko vo maghroor-e-khud-aara jaane hai
Aashiq sa toh saada koi aur na hoga duniya mein
Ji ke ziyaan ko ishq mein usske apna vaara jaane hai
Chaaragari bimaari-e-dil ki rasm-e-shahr-e-husn nahin
Varna dilbar-e-naadaan bhi iss dard ka chaara jaane hai

Mehr-o-vafaa-o-lutf-o-inaayat ek se vaaqif in mein nahin
Aur toh sab kuchh tanz-o-kinaaya ramz-o-ishaara jaane hai
Tishna-e-khoon hai apna kitna 'Mir' bhi naadaan talkhi-kash
Dum-daar aab-e-tegh ko uss ke aab-e-gavaara jaane hai

Every leaf, every shrubbery is of the reality of my being aware
except for the flower the entire garden knows of the affair
Oh my God! Oh my God! I cry before the one so fair
but my godless narcissist does not care
None on the planet is as naive as a lover
who is happy to lose his heart and enjoys to suffer
To care for the heart in pain is not her concern
although the remedy simple is known even to the innocent I so yearn
Loyalty, care, grace and love for one—she is indifferent to all
just teasing and taunting, accusing and blaming is her call
Thirsty for your own blood how silly and masochistic, Mir, can you be
to accept the shimmering sharp sword of the beloved as elixir with glee?

Ulti ho gayin sab tadbeerein kuchh na davaa ne kaam kiya
dekha iss bimaar-e-dil ne aakhir kaam tamaam kiya
Ahd-e-javaani ro ro kaataa peeri mein linn aankhein moond
yaani raat bahut thhe jaage subah hui aaraam kiya
Naahaq hum majbooron par yeh tohmat hai mukhtaari ki
chaahte hain so aap karein hain hum ko bas badnaam kiya
Saare rind aubaash jahaan ke tujh se sujud mein rehte hain
baanke tedhe tirchhe tikhe sab ka tujh ko imaam kiya
Sarzad hum se be-adabi toh vahshat mein bhi kam hi hui
koson uss ki ore gaye par sajda har har gaam kiya
Kis ka kaaba kaisa qibla kaun haram hai kya ehraam
kooche ke uss ke baashindon ne sab ko yahin se salaam kiya
Yaan ke sapiid-o-siyah mein hum ko dakhl jo hai so itna hai
Raat ko ro ro subah kiya ya din ko juua tuun shaam kiya
Subah chaman mein uss ko kahin takleef-e-havaa le aaithi
Rukh se gul ko mol liya qaamat se sarv ghulaam kiya
Saad-e-siimiin donon uss ke haath meiin la kar chhodh diye
Bhoole uss ke qaul-o-qasam par haayai khayaal-e-khaam kiya
'Mir' ke deen-o-mazhab ko ab poochhte kya ho un ne toh

Qashqa kheencha dair meiin baitha kab ka tark islaam kiya

All propositions are overturned no prescription is of help,
see how the sick heart has done me in at every step
My youth was spent whining when age caught up the eyes closed,
like after a wakeful night, the day is wasted as if stoned
In vain the vulnerable are accused of being in charge,
it is what the godly beloved wants that is done, my life is needlessly seen as large
Everyone the caring and the carefree, the doubting and the double-crossing all hold you in awe,
The silly, the stupid, the smart and the skilful before you bow
Even at the peak of my obsession I did not lose my cool,
I stalked her for miles but at every step prostrated as a rule
Which Ka'aba, what Mecca where is the land of pure,
those in her neighbourhood prefer to prostrate here for sure
Here in the light and darkness of existence this is our only control,
to spend the night sobbing into dawn, and dawn somehow stretch to twilight is the only goal

Painful winds breezed her into the garden one morn,
I won the flower over with a look, and my poise made the cypress tall one a slave born
I took into my hands her lovely, silver-white wrist then let it go,
Only because I had forgotten her false promises and vows, and silly plans though.
Why question Mir's faith and belief now that he has, marked his forehead with sandal powder, sat in a temple and turned his back on Islam, alas!

Kya kahoon tumse main ki kya hai ishq
Jaan ka rog hai balaa hai ishq
Ishq hi ishq hai jahaan dekho
Saare aalam mein bhar raha hai ishq
Ishq hai tarz-o-taur ishq ke taiin
Kahin banda kahin khuda hai ishq
Ishq maashooq ishq aashiq hai
Yaanii apna hi mubtalaa hai ishq
Hai humaare bhi taur ka aashiq
Jis kisi ko kahin hua hai ishq
Koi khvaahaan nahin mohabbat ka
Tu kahe jins-e-naa-ravaa hai ishq
'Mir' ji zard hote jaate ho
Kya kahin tum ne bhi kiya hai ishq

What should I say to you what is love
Disease of the soul and evil spirit is love

There is love as far as the eye can see
overwhelming all of life is love
Love is its own law
a creature there and the creator here are both love
Love is beloved love is lover
love engrossed in the self is love
That lover is like me
Whoever, where ever he has been in love, is love
Those who desire not love
tell you how undesirable is love
Mir Ji how jaundiced you are becoming
Is it true that you have also discovered love?

3. Ghulam Hamdani Mushafi (1751–1824)

Ghazal

Khwaab thha ya khayaal thha kya thha
Hijr thha ya visaal thha kya thha
Mere pehlu mein raat jaa-kar vo
Maah thha ya hilaal thha kya thha
Chamki bijli si par na samjhe hum
Husn thha ya jamaal thha kya thha
Shab jo dil do do haath uchhalta thha
Vajd thha ya voh haal thha kya thha
Jisko hum roz-e-hijr samjhe thhe
Maah thha ya voh saal thha kya thha
'Mushafi' shab jo chup tu baitha thha
Kya tujhe kuchh malaal thha kya thha

Was it a dream or reverie, what was it?
Was it absence or presence, what was it?
The night spent in my arms
Was it the full moon or crescent, what was it?
Thunder-loud warnings I did not heed
Was it beauty was it goodness, what was it?
The evening when the heart skipped many a beat
Was it real or unreal, what was it?
What seemed like a daily loss
Was it month or year, what was it?
'Mushafi', the evening you sat so quiet
Was it regret, what was it?

Log kehte hain mohabbat mein asar hota hai
Kaun se sheher mein hota hai kidhar hota hai
Usske kooche mein hai nit surat-e-bedaad nai
Qatl har khasta baa-andaaz-e-digar hota hai
Nahin maaloom ki maatam hai falaq par kiska
Roz kyun chaak girebaan-e-seher hota hai
Wahin yun hi apni bhi hai baareek-tar-az-mu gardan
Tegh ke saath yahaan zikr-e-kamar hota hai
Karke main yaad dil apne ko bahut rota hun
Jab kisi shakhs ka duniya se safar hota hai
Uski mizhgaan ka koi naam na lo kya haasil
Mera in baaton se suraakh jigar hota hai
'Mushafi' hum toh tere milne ko aaye kayi baar
Ae deewane tu kisi vaqt bhi ghar hota hai

I am told that love is divine
In which place is it so, where is it so?
Every day I am abused in the beloved's home
Destroyed in different ways
Don't know who the heavens mourn
And who tatters dawn every morn
The neck is placed in a position delicate
I wish all talk of the sword around the waist did sit
Thought of my heart makes me bawl
When the worldly journey of a human being has a fall
Mention not her eyelashes, what is the use?
Such talk ruptures the soul like abuse
'Mushafi' I came to see you often
When are you ever home, you crazy person?

Aaye ho toh yeh hijaab kya hai
Munh khol do naqaab kya hai
Seene mein theherta hii nahin dil
Ya-Rabb isse iztiraab kya hai
Kal tegh nikaal mujh se bola
tu dekh toh iss ki aab kya hai
Maaloom nahin ki apna divaan
hai marsiya ya kitaab kya hai
Jo mar gai maare lutf hi ke
phir un pe miyaan itaab kya hai
Auron se toh hai yeh be-hijaabi
mujh se hii tujhe hijaab kya hai
Ae 'Mushafi' uth yeh dhoop aayi

Itna bhi diwaane khwaab kya hai

Now that you are here why the veil?
Show me your face, do away with the cover
without fail
The heart refuses to rest in the chest
Oh Lord! what is this restlessness? Tell me what is best
Yesterday the sharp blade appeared to ask me
witness the splendour, and my shine see
Unknown is my word
What is the lamentation what is my book I know not
Those dead died out of sheer joy
Why then, dear, mourn death?
Others are allowed your immodesty
then why be modest with me?
O Mushafi, wake up now that the sun shines
your dreams cannot be so obsessive, so fine.

4. Khwaja Haidar Ali 'Aatish' (1778–1847)

Ghazal

Buth-khaana todiye masjid ko dhaaiye
Dil ko na todiye yeh khuda ka maqaam hai
Ajab teri hai ae yeh mehboob soorat
Nazar se gir gaye sab khoobsoorat
Ae sanam jisne tujhe chaand si soorat di hai
Ussi Allah ne mujhko bhi mohabbat di hai
Napaak hoga kabhi husn-o-ishq ka jhagda

Vo kissa hai yeh ki jiska koi gavaah nahin
Sunn toh sahi jahaan mein hai tera fasaana kya
Kehti hai tujhko khalq-e-khuda ga-ibaana kya

Tear down the temple, demolish the mosque
Break not the heart, home of the beloved
Extraordinary is the lover's beauty
All other loveliness pales away in front of it
The one who gave you moon-like beauty
The same creator gave me love
Favour not feud between beauty and love
It is an experience without witness
Listen to the legends spread about you
The world believes that you are not you.
The poet refers to the cruel world spreading rumours about the beloved.

Shab-e-vasl thhi chaandni ka samaan thha
Baghal mein sanam thha khuda meherbaan thha
Mubaarak shab-e-qadr se bhi vo shab thhi
Seher tak mah o mushtari ka qiraan thha
Vo shab thhi ki thhi raushni jismein din ki
Zamiin par se ik noor ta aasmaan thha
Nikaale thhe do chaand uss ne muqaabil
Vo shab subah-e-jannat ka jis par gumaan thha
Aruusii ki shab ki halaavat thhi haasil
Farah-naak thhi rooh dil shaadmaan thha
Mushahid jamaal-e-pari ki thhi aankhein
Makaan-e-visaal ik tilismi makaan thha

Huzoori nigaahon ko deedaar se thhi
Khula thha vo parda ki jo darmiyaan thha
Kiya thha usse bosa-baazi ne paida
Kamar ki tarah se jo gha.eb dahaan thha
Haqeeqat dikhaata thha ishq-e-majaazi
Nihaan jis ko samjhe hue thhe ayaan thha
Bayaan khvaab ki tarah jo kar raha hai
Yeh kissa hai jabka ki 'Aatish' javaan thha

The meeting was bathed in moonlight
Beside me the beloved, and merciful was the creator
More auspicious was the evening than the Night of Revelation
When the Moon and Jupiter remained engaged till dawn
What an evening it was sparkling like the light of day
Bright as paradise on earth
Two moons appeared one after the other
The night stretching into heavenly morn
The sweetness of having become one
Spirits high and the heart happy
Witnessed by the wondrous eyes of beauty
In a magical abode
The look yearning to pay homage to appearance
The veil dropped from in between
Born of kisses
Whose waist dissolved like the mouth
Imagined love turned to reality
What was puzzle became plain
This told like a dream by one
Is a story from when he was very young.

5. Insha Allah Khan (1752–1817)

Ghazal

Mil mujhse ae pari tujhe Quran ki qasam
Deta hun tujhko takht-e-sulaimaan ki qasam
Karr-o-bayon ki tujhko qasam aur 'arsh' ki
Jibril ki qasam tujhe rizvaan ki qasam
Tuuba ki salsabil ki kausar ke jaam ki
Ruhul-qudus ki tujhko qasam aur masih ki
Mariyam ke tujhko iffat-e-daamaan ki qasam
Tauret ki qasam qasam injil ki tujhe
Tujhko qasam zabur ki furqaan ki qasam
Tujhko Muhammad-e-arabi ki qasam hai aur
Maula-Ali ki shah-e-khurasaan ki qasam
Millat mein jiski tu hui uss ki qasam tujhe
Aur apne deen mazhab-o-imaan ki qasam
Daamaan ko mere haath se uss raat mat jhatak
Tujh ko seher ke chaak-e-garebaan ki qasam
Muddat se teri chaah-e-zaqan mein ghariq hun
Billah mujhko yusuf-e-kanaan ki qasam
Kaidi hun main tera ba-khuda-vandi-e-khuda
Aur uss aziz-e-misr ke zindaan ki qasam
Muusa ki hai qasam tujhe aur koh-e-tur ki
Noor-o-farogh-e-jalva-e-lamaan ki qasam
Nargis ki aankh ki qasam aur gul ke kaan ki
Tujhko sar-e-aziz-e-gulistaan ki qasam
Tujhko qasam hai ghuncha-e-zambaq ke naak ki
Aur shor-e-andalib-e-ghazal-khvaan ki qasam
Sone ki gaaye ki qasam aur rud-e-nil ki

Firaun ki qasam tujhe haamaan ki qasam
Bistar mira hai khar-e-mughiilaan basaan-e-qais
Laila ki hai tujhe saf-e-mizhgaan ki qasam
Aisi badi qasam bhi na maane to hai tujhe
Tujh ko usi ke shaukat-e-zishaan ki qasam
Dev-e-safed ki qasam aur koh-e-qaaf ki
Baagh-e-iram ki aur paristaan ki qasam
Lonaa-chamaari ki qasam aur kallu-abir ki
Kaali-balaa ki ghul-e-bayaabaan ki qasam
Qasmein toh saari ho chukin baaqi hai ab
Peepal taley ke bhutne ki shaitaan ki qasam
Haan phir tu kahiyo haai voh kis tarah hue ghazab
'Insha' na chhedh mujhko meri jaan ki qasam

Promise me by the Quran that you will come to me you beauty
Give me your word in the name of the throne of King Solomon
Swear by all creation, swear by the heavens
Swear by archangel Gabriel, swear by the gatekeeper of paradise
Swear by the fragrant trees, the fountains and rivers of paradise
Swear by all pure of soul and the messiah
Swear by the modesty of mother Mary's hemline
Swear by the Torah, by the New Testament promise
Swear by the Book of David, the Book of Truth
Swear by Muhammad the Arab
Swear by Maula Ali, the King of Khorasan
Swear by the community you belong to

And by your belief, religion and faith
Don't snatch away the shawl from my hand that night
Swear by dawn's tattered neckline
For long I have been drowned in the depth of your dimple
By God I swear by Joseph of Cannan
I am your prisoner I swear by the godliness of God
and swear by the prison of that favourite of Egypt
Promise me by Moses and swear by the mountain of the burning bush
Swear by the spreading radiance of light
Swear by the eyes of the daffodil, and the ears of the rose
Swear by all that is lovable in a garden
Swear by the nose of the iris
Swear by the orchestra of nightingales
Swear by the golden cow and by the River Nile,
swear by Haman, the cruel minister of the pharaoh
My bedding of thorn bushes like that of Qais, the obsessed Majnun
Give me your word in the name of Laila's eyelashes
If this is a promise beyond you
Swear by an obsession similar
Promise me in the name of the white giant and the mountain Qaf
Swear by paradise and by the land of fairies
Swear by the sorceress Lona Chamari and by Kallu Abir's
Black magic in the wilderness

All the swearing is done except
For the evil demons under the fig tree
Now you will say how wicked you are
'Insha', don't tease me, I swear upon my life let me be.

Neend maston ko kahaan aur kidhar ka takiya
Khisht-e-khum-khana hai yaan apne toh sar ka takiya
Lakht-e-dil aa ke musafir se theherte hain yahaan
Chashm hai humse gadaaon ki guzar ka takiya
Jis taraf aankh utha dekhiye ho jaaye asar
Hum toh rakhte hain faqat apni nazar ka takiya
Chain hargiz nahin makhmal ke usse takiye par
Uss pari ke liye ho hoor ke par ka takiya
Sar toh chaahe hai mera hove mayassar tere
Haath ka baazu ka zaanu ka qamar ka takiya
Yeh toh haasil hai kahaan bhej de lekin mujhko
Jis mein baalon ki ho boo tere ho sar ka takiya
Tikhe-pan ke tere qurbaan akad ke sadqe
Kya hi baitha hai laga kar ke sipar ka takiya
Garche hum sakht gunahgar hain lekin vallaah
Dil mein jo dar hai humein hai ussi dar ka takiya
Girya o aah-o-fughan naala o ya rab fariyaad
Sab ko hai har shab-o-roz apne asar ka takiya
Dhoondhte kab hain pidar aur pisar ka takiya
Gar bharosa hai humein ab toh bharosa tera
Aur takiya hai agar tere hi dar ka takiya
Shauq se soiye sar rakh ke mere zaanu par
Uss ko mat samajhiye kuchh khauf-o-khatar ka takiya
Jab talak aap na jayenge rahega yun hi

Sarkega tab hi ki jab kahiyega sarka takiya
Lutf-e-izadi hi se ummeed hai Insha-allah
Kuchh nahin rakhte hain hum fazl-o-hunar ka takiya

What is sleep for the intoxicated? No question of a pillow
A brick of the tavern cushions the head
A piece of the heart of every traveller is left here
Have-nots look for comfort of a pillow from the likes of us
Wherever the look rests there it is
The only pillow that I carry is that of my vision
There is no comfort on a pillow of velvet
That fairy is deserving of a pillow made from the wings of angels
My head would love to have your kind of comfort
Like a pillow of hands, arms, lap and waist
It is possible, but where should I be sent
Where the fragrance is that of your hair and a pillow of your brow
Crazy about your coquetry appreciative of your arrogance
I sit using a shield as a pillow
If I am a sinner by God
The fear in my heart is also the fear I use as a pillow
Sobbing, sighing, complaining, pleading, 'Oh God! Help!'
Everyone every day wonders what kind of pillow will come their way
The irresponsible and the carefree have left the neighbourhood
No longer interested in a father and son pillow

If I have faith, that faith is in you
And if there is a pillow it is a pillow of the fear of you
With pleasure sleep with the head on my lap
Don't look upon it as a pillow of fright or danger
It will remain the way it is till you leave
It will slip only when you say the pillow slips
Pleasure divine is the only hope, God willing,
In my possession is nothing but a pillow of virtue
and vision.

6. Imam Baksh Nasikh (1772–1838)

Couplets

Zindagi zinda-dili ka hai naam
Murda-dil khaak jiya karte hain

Hearts full of life are alive
Lifeless hearts do not live

Teri soorat se kisi ki nahin milti soorat
Hum jahaan mein teri tasveer liye phirte hain

No one else is like you
I wander around the world with your image

Vo nahin bhoolta jahaan jaun
Haaye main kya karun kahaan jaun

I am unable to forget you wherever I go
Sigh! What do I do? Where do I go?

Siyah-bakhti mein kab koi kisi ka saath deta hai
Ki tariki mein saaya bhi juda rehta hai insaan se

In times difficult no one stays
When darkness falls, even the shadow of man disappears

Aane mein sada der lagaate hi rahe tum
Jaate rahe hum jaan se aate hi rahe tum

You always took your time to come
Life kept ebbing out of me and you kept saying I am coming

Justuju karni har ek amr mein naadaani hai
Jo ki peshaani pe likhi hai voh pesh aani hai

Foolish to be concerned about every affair
Whatever is fated will come to pass, beware!

Dariya-e-husn aur bhi do haath badh gaya
Angdai ussne nashe mein lii jab utha ke haath

How the river of beauty overflowed
when unconsciously she lifted the arms to stretch

Mashooqon se ummeed-e-vafaa rakhte ho 'Nasikh'
Naadaan koi duniya mein nahin tum se zyada

You expect the beloved to be faithful, 'Nasikh',
None other in the world is more naïve than you

Tamaam umr yun hi ho gayi basar apni
Shab-e-firaaq gayi roz-e-intizaar aaya

My entire life passed by just like that
The night passed in longing and the day in wait

Lete lete karvatein tujh bin jo ghabraata hun main
Naam le le kar tera raaton ko chillata hun main

Tossing in bed without you worries me alright
I shriek repeatedly your name all night

Ae ajal ek din aakhir tujhe aana hai vale
Aaj aati shab-e-furqat mein toh ehsaan hota

Oh end, you will come eventually but
It would be a favour if you come on the night of separation

Gaya voh chhodh kar raaste mein mujhko
Ab uss ka naqsh-e-pa hai aur main hun

He has left me behind on the way
Now his footprints are there and I am.

Jis qadar hum se tum hue nazdeek
Uss qadar duur kar diya humko

The closer you got to me
The further you made me feel from you

Kis tarah chhodun yakaayak teri zulfon ka khayaal
Ek muddat ke yeh kaale naag hain paale hue

How do I let go instantly the thought of your tresses?
It took eons to tame your serpentine curls

Furqat-e-yar mein insaan hun main ya ki sahaab
Har baras aake rula jaati hai barsaat mujhe

Abandoned by the beloved am I a human being or a cloud?
That every season the monsoons come to make me cry

Ghazal

Sau qisson se behtar hai kahaani mere dil ki
Sunn uss ko tu ae jaan zabaani mere dil ki
Har naale mein yaan tukde jigar hota hai bulbul

Aasaan nahin tarz udaani mere dil ki
Honi hai shahid ek na ik roz tamanna
Mauquf ho kya marsiya-khvaani mere dil ki
Peer mein bhi milta hai jo kamsin koi mehboob
Karti hai vahin udd jawaani mere dil ki
Taqseem kiye paara-e-dil bazm-e-butaan mein
Har ek ke hai paas nishaani mere dil ki
Ik baat mein ho jaaiye musakhkhar vo pari-ru
Sunta hi nahin sehr-bayaani mere dil ki
Hai abr toh kya chaahe falak ko bhi jala de
Bijli mein kahaan shola-fishaani mere dil ki
Zulfon mein kiya qaid na aabru se kiya qatl
Tu ne toh koi baat na maani mere dil ki
Yeh baar-e-gham-e-ishq samaaya hai ki 'Nasikh'
Hai koh se dah-chand giraani mere dil ki

Better than hundred other stories is the story of my heart
Listen to it, sweetheart, in the language of my heart
With every call, the inside of the nightingale chips
Easy is not the style of narration of my heart
One day desire will elevate itself to wisdom
Till then should the lamentation be postponed of my heart
Even in old age when a youthful lover is found
There and then wakes up the youth of the heart
The assembly of idols tears the heart into pieces
Each one is in possession of a piece of my heart
A sentence conquers the angel face
But deaf she is to the magical narration of my heart

So what if it is a cloud? It can singe skies
Lightning does not compare with the flame of my heart
Your locks did not imprison me, your eyebrows did not slay me
You did not heed any desire of my heart
This burden of grief of love is so powerful, Nasikh
Ten times more than a mountain does it weigh upon my heart.

7. Qalandar Baksh Jurat (1748–1809)

Ghazal

Ab ishq tamaasha mujhe dikhlaaye hai kuchh aur
Kehta hoon kuchh aur munh se nikal jaaye hai kuchh aur
Naaseh ki himaaqat toh zara dekhiyo yaaron
Samjha hoon main kuchh aur mujhe samjhaaye hai kuchh aur
Kya deeda-e-hhoon-baar se nisbat hai ki yeh abr
Barsaaye hai kuchh aur voh barsaaye kuchh aur
Rone de hansaa mujhko na hamdam ki tujhe ab
Kuchh aur hii bhaata hai mujhe bhaaye hai kuchh aur
Paighambar aaya hai yeh ausaan ganvaaye
Poochhoon hoon main kuchh aur mujhe batlaaye hai kuchh aur
'Jurat' ki tarah mere havaas ab nahin bar ja
Kehta hoon kuchh aur munh se nikal jaaye hai kuchh aur

Love is now a different tale
I want to say something, but something else is what I wail
What ill advice from a friend
I know something and he wants me to something else pretend
Is this related to tears or is a drink?
Something rains but it rains something else he thinks
Let me cry, do not make me laugh now
I need something and something else for you is wow
The message to me is to forget
I ask for something and something else is what I get
I desire no longer like 'Jurat', go away
I want to say something but something else is what I say.

Baithe toh paas hain par aankh uthaa sakte nahin
Ji laga hai par abhi haath laga sakte nahin
Door se dekh voh lab kaat-te hain apne honth
Hai abhi paas-e-adab honth hila sakte nahin
Takte hain uss qad o rukhsar ko hasrat se aur aah
Bhench kar khuub sa chhaati se laga sakte nahin
Dil toh inn paanv pe laute hai mera vaqt-e-khiram
Shab ko duzdi se bhi par unko daba sakte nahin
Chor se raat khade rehte hain iss dar se lage
Par jo matlub hai voh jins chura sakte nahin
Rijhte un ki adaaon pe hain kya kya lekin
Maare andeshe ke gardan bhi hilaa sakte nahin
Dekh rehte hain voh aaina-e-zaanu usska
Par kisi shakl se zaanu ko bhidaa sakte nahin

Qayede kya hamein maaloom nahin ulfat ke
Be-kam-o-kaast magar unko padhaa sakte nahin
Chipke tak rehte hain rang uss ka bhabuka sa hum
Aah par dil ki lagi apni bujha sakte nahin
Kya ghazab hai ki vahi bole toh bole az-khud
Hum unhein kyunki bulaven ki bulaa sakte nahin
Garche hum-khana hain 'Jurat' pe humaare aise
Bakht soye ki kahin saath sulaa sakte nahin

Beside me so near you sit but look I cannot
The heart wants to but the hand cannot
Watching from afar I see the mouth bite the lips
Out of self-respect my own lips move I cannot
I look at the height of beauty with longing, sigh
Tightly hold her to my chest I cannot
The heart has slowly wriggled down to the feet
even at night grab an embrace I cannot
Like a thief in the dark I lean at the doorstep
but steal the desired one I cannot
Floored by her coquetry
but filled with doubts even shake my head I cannot
I watch her thighs
but touch my thigh to hers, no way I cannot
As if I know not the lessons of love
but teach her the lessons I cannot
I cling to her like the red of her face
sigh but the flame of my heart snuff I cannot
What is this that she alone speaks at will
how do I call her when call her I cannot
I am of the same species as you, Jurat

other species are allowed to sleep together, with you I cannot.

8. Saadat Yaar Khan Rangin (1757–1835)

Ghazal

Ishq se bach ke kidhar jayenge hum
Hai yeh maujood jidhar jayenge hum
Tan ke bas rakhiye qabza par haath
Dekhiye muft mein dar jayenge hum
Teri dehleez par apne sar ko
Ek din kaatke dhar jayenge hum
Vo yeh kehte hain na de dil hum ko
Dekh lete hi mukar jayenge hum
Manaa karte ho ab bas yaaro aaj
Usske ghar jaayenge par jayenge hum
Dil ki leni hai khabar humko zaroor
Aaj toh phir bhi udhar jayenge hum
Dum kahin lenge na phir taa-ba-adam
Tere koocha se agar jayenge hum
Tu na guzrega jafaa se zaalim
Jaan se apni guzar jayenge hum
Zeest baaki hai toh apna 'Rangin'
Naam iss ishq mein kar jayenge hum

Where can I hide from love? It is wherever I go
Carefully caress the body without frightening me so
On your doorstep my head one day I will lay
Don't give me your heart, they say

I will refuse, and that will be the day
You refuse, 'That is enough for the day,' you say
I will go to the house, I will, to find out if the heart beats still
I will not rest if your home I don't see
You may not know such pain
My life however will end in vain
If life is left then your 'Rangin'
Will make eternal my love for you, my queen.

9. Wajid Ali Shah 'Akhtar' (1822–1887)

Ghazal

Ghuncha-e-dil khile jo chaho tum
Gulshan-e-dehr mein sabaa ho tum
Bemuravvat ho bevafaa ho tum
Apne matlab ke aashnaa ho tum
Kaun ho kya ho kya tumhein likhein
Aadmi ho pari ho kya ho tum
Pista-e-lab se hum ko quvvat do
Dil-e-bimaar ki davaa ho tum
Ussi Akhtar ke tum hue mashooq
Hanso bolo ussi ko chaho tum

The heart will bloom if you like
In the garden of the world you are the morning breeze
you are faithless, you are inconsiderate,
you are a friend of your own interest

Who you are, what you are, what should I write
about you?
Human, fairy—what are you?
Empower me with your pistachio-shaped mouth
Cure of the ailing heart, you are
beloved of Akhtar
Laugh, speak, love, only him.

10. Mir Babar Ali Anees (1803–1873)

Couplets

Ashiq ko dekhte hain dupatte ko taan kar
Dete hain humko sharbat-e-deedar chhaan kar

Spying on the lover from behind a veil
offering sieved glimpses to intoxicate

Ashk-e-gham diida-e-pur-nam se sambhaale na gaye
Yeh voh bachhe hain jo maa baap se paale na gaye

Tearful eyes filled with sorrow could not nurture them
these are children whose parents could not care for
them

Tamaam umr jo ki hum se be-rukhi sab ne
Kafan mein hum bhi azizon se munh chhupa ke chale

All my life because indifferent to me were all friends
I too hid myself from loved ones behind a shroud in the end.

'Anees' aasaan nahin aabaad karna ghar mohabbat ka
Yeh unka kaam hai jo zindagi barbaad karte hain

'Anees', it is not easy to nurture love's home
This is the job of those who destroy life.

Ghazal

Ishaare kya nigah-e-naaz-e-dilrubaa ke chale
Sitam ke teer chale nimche qazaa ke chale
Gunah ka bojh jo gardan pe hum uthaa ke chale
Khuda ke aage khajalat se sar jhukaa ke chale
Talab se aar hai Allah se faqiron ko
Kahin jo ho gaya phera sada sunaa ke chale
Pukaare kehti thhi hasrat se naash aashiq ki
Sanam kidhar ko hamein khaak mein milaa ke chale
Misal-e-mahi-e-be-ab maujein tadpa kiin
Habaab phoot ke royei jo tum nahaa ke chale
Maqaam yun hua iss kaar-gaah-e-duniya mein
Ki jaise din ko musafir saraa mein aa ke chale
Kisi ka dil na kiya hum ne paemaal kabhi
Chale jo raah toh chyunthi ko bhi bachaa ke chale
Mila jinhein unheen uftaadgi se auj mila
Unhin ne khaai hai thokar jo sar uthaa ke chale

'Anees' dam ka bharosa nahin thahar jao
Charaagh le ke kahaan saamne hawaa ke chale

The coquettish glances the beloved flung
Arrows of cruelty justice by dagger flung
The weight of sins upon my neck flung
Before God my head full of shame flung
Paupers are ashamed of expecting so much from God
Begging everywhere their cries flung
The corpse of the lover calls out with longing
Beloved, where to, after having me to dust flung
Like fish out of water the waves thrashed
Droplets burst into tears seeing you in your bath flung
The situation is such in the workshop of life
Like a traveller in a guest house is forever flung
Have never hurt a heart
Even made way for the ant on the path flung
Those who received endless sorrow
Are those who have walked with the head high
flung.
Anees, life is uncertain, wait!
To the winds the lamp you have flung.

Marsiya

Dasht-e-viga mein noor-e-khuda ka zuhur hai
zarron mein raushni-e-tajalli-e-tur hai
Ik aftaab-e-rukh ki ziya duur duur hai
Koson zameen aks se dariya-e-noor hai

Allah-re husn tabqa-e-ambar-sarisht ka
Maidaan-e-karbala hai namuna bahisht ka

The desert is illuminated by light of the creator of the world
Each particle of sand is a manifestation of the divine mountain of Moses
The light from a sun-like countenance spreads far
For miles the earth shimmers like a river of light
Oh God, the level of the beauty of his fragrance converts the battlefield of Karbala into a piece of paradise.

11. Mirza Salaamat Ali Dabeer (1803–1835)

Marsiya

Kis sher ki aamad hai ki rann kaanp raha hai
Rustam ka jigar zer-e-kafan kaanp raha hai
Har qasr-e-salaatin-e-zaman kaanp raha hai
Sab ek taraf charkha-e-kuhan kaanp raha hai
Shamshir-ba-kaf dekh ke Haider ke pisar ko
Jibreel lazartey hain sametey hue par ko

What lion has arrived to make the desert shudder
To make Rustom in his shroud shiver
Kingdoms of different eras shudder
On one side the skies shiver
Seeing sword in the hand of Haider's son
Makes angel Gabriel fold his wings and shudder.